THE WISDOM OF THE EGYPTIANS

Brian Brown

British Library Cataloguing in Publication Data

A catalogue record for this book is available from the British Library

ISBN-13: 978-1-909735-04-0

Printed and bound in Great Britain by Lightning Source UK Ltd., 6 Precedent Drive, Rooksley, Milton Keynes MK13 8PR.

Cover Illustration: *Osiris, Isis & Nephthys*.
Papyrus of Hunefer. 19th Dynasty (*circa* 1285 BC)

CONTENTS

INTRODUCTION

In ancient times the land that is now called Egypt was called by the people, then inhabiting that part of Africa, "Kam," a word that means "black" or "dark-colored" and referred to the dark color of the muddy soil in their land. To the Hebrews this name was known as "Khám" or "Ham" and in the Bible the Egyptians are referred to as "Sons of Ham" or "Children of Ham."

These people had a God called "Ptah" to whom they raised a temple - the temple was called "He-Ka-ptah" or House of "Ka" - of "Ptah." This name, that was in the beginning confined to "Memphis," gradually spread to other parts of the Nile Valley, and by degrees the whole country became known as "HeKapath," to other people with whom these people had contact.

The Greeks changed the name into "Aiguptos" and the Romans changed it into "Aegyptus," so from these names we get the name in its present form - "Egypt," To what race do the Egyptians belong? On this subject Prof. James Breasted in his "History of Egypt" writes the following:

"On the now bare and windswept desert plateau, through which the Nile has hollowed its channel, there once dwelt a race of men. Plenteous rains, now no longer known there, rendered it a fertile and productive region. The geological changes which have since made the country almost rainless, denuded it of vegetation and soil, and made it for the most part uninhabitable, took place many thousands of years before the beginning of the Egyptian civilization, which we are to study; but the prehistoric race, who before these changes peopled the plateau, left behind them as the sole memorial of their existence vast numbers of rude flint implements, now lying scattered about the surface of the present desert exposed by denudation.

"These men of the paleolithic age were the first inhabitants of whom we have any knowledge in Egypt. They cannot be connected in any way with the historic or prehistoric civilization of the Egyptians and they fall exclusively within the province of the geologist and anthropologist. The forefathers of the people with whom we shall have to deal were related to the Libyans or North Africans on the one hand, and on the other to the peoples of eastern Africa, now known as the Galla, Somali, Bega and other tribes.

"An invasion of the Nile Valley by Semitic Nomads of Asia, stamped its essential character unmistakably upon the language of the African people there. The earliest strata of the language accessible to us, betray clearly this composite origin. While still colored by its African antecedents, the language is in structure Semitic. It is moreover a completed product as observable in our earliest preserved examples of it; but the fusion of the Libyans and East Africans with the Nile Valley peoples continued far into historic times, and in the case of the Libyans may be traced in ancient historical documents for three thousand years or more.

"The Semitic immigration from Asia, examples of which are also observable in the historic age, occurred in an epoch that lies far below our remotest historical horizon. We shall never be able to determine when, nor with certainty through what channels, it took place, although the most probable route is that along which we may observe a similar influx from the deserts of Arabia in historic times, the isthmus of Suez, by which the Mohammedan invasion entered the country.

"While the Semitic language which they brought with them left its indelible impress upon the old Nile Valley people, the nomadic life of the desert which the invaders left behind them, evidently was not so persistent, and the religion of Egypt, that element of life which always receives the stamp of its environment, shows no trace of the desert life. The affinities observable in the language are confirmed in case of the Libyans, by the surviving products of archaic civilization in the Nile Valley such as some of the early pottery, which closely resembles that still made by the Libyan Kabyles. Again the representations of the early Puntites, or Somali people, on the Egyptian monuments, show striking resemblances to the Egyptians themselves. The examination of the bodies exhumed from archaic burials in the Nile Valley, which we had hoped might bring further evidence f or the settlement of the problem, has, however, produced such diversity of opinion among the physical anthropologists, as to render it impossible for the historian to obtain decisive results from their researches. The conclusion once maintained by some historians, that the Egyptian was of African negro origin is now refuted; and evidently indicated that at most he may have been slightly tinctured with negro blood, in addition to other ethnic elements already mentioned."

THE EGYPTIAN RELIGION

If we were called upon to characterize the Egyptian religion in a few words, we should call it, both as a system and as a cult, an almost monarchical polytheism in a theocratic form. The Egyptian polytheism was not purely monarchical, for there were several divine monarchies; and only by the somewhat arbitrary doctrine that all the chief gods were in reality the same under different names, could the semblance of monarchy be maintained. But this religion was undoubtedly theocratic in the strictest sense of the word. The divinity himself reigned through his son, the absolute king, his incarnation and representative on earth. The priesthood of Amon, strengthened by its victory over the heretic, and by the measureless wealth which the munificence of successful conquerors poured into its lap, had attained the most tremendous power in the state; and when, after a long time, its members had reduced the king to weak tools in their hands, and succeeded at last in usurping the throne itself, the theocracy was altered in form only, but not in its essence. The place of the king highpriest was taken by the highpriest-king. But even this change was of short duration. Against another power no less favored by the kings of the new empire, the power of the army (composed for the greater part of hired foreign troops), the priestly princes proved unable to keep their ground. They had to leave the country, and in Ethiopia they founded a new sacerdotal kingdom. Still the rule of the kings, who sprang from this military revolution, was purely theocratic.

But this only characterizes the form of the Egyptian religion. If we search for the leading thought, contained in all its myths and symbols, and in all its institutions and ceremonies, it may best be comprised in the word "life." The sign of life (ankh) is the holiest and the most commonly used of all the symbols. The gods bear it in their hands, hold it to the lips of their worshippers, and pour it out in streams over the heads of their favorites. For they actually give life, now by the light which they continually cause to triumph over the powers of darkness, again by the regular recurrence of the fructifying waters, or by mysterious operations in the centre of the earth. And hence they set such store on the possession of the lawful king. He, the son of the sun, was the living pledge that these blessings should not cease. His coronation was an agricultural festival, the beginning of the harvest; his greatest care was to spread the waters of the Nile through canals as far as possible over the fields. From this arose also their great fear of death and eternal darkness, and the efforts and sacrifices which they made to secure an eternal existence, either in the fertile land of Osiris, or as a follower of the god of light, and, as it is put, "to obtain the crown of life."

Entirely swayed by these ideas, the Egyptian, although his religious thinking did not stand still, clung to the existing state of things; he did not relinquish what was old. He may have connected different ideas with it; but the holy texts which he muttered during the Ptolemean era were often the same as those his ancestors had uttered at the altars and the tombs more than thirty centuries ago. The nature of the land which bore and fed him had imprinted a peculiar stamp on his religion. Moreover, his religion became to him more and more the only thing of supreme value. Treasures, the fruits of his industry, and all the skill which was the product of his remarkable civilization, he spent on the building and the decorating of his tombs and temples. Those of Amon at Thebes gradually became the largest in the world. His whole literature, even that which was not destined for a religious purpose, is, with a few exceptions, saturated by a religious spirit.

Many of the virtues which we are apt to suppose a monopoly of Christian culture appear as the ideal of these old Egyptians. Brugsch says a thousand voices from the tombs of Egypt declare this. One inscription in upper Egypt says: "He loved his father, he honored his mother, he loved his brethren, and never went from his home in bad-temper. He never preferred the great man to the low one." Another says: "I was a wise man, my soul loved God. I was a brother to the great men and a father to the humble ones, and never was a mischief-maker." An inscription at Sais, on a priest who lived in the sad days of Camybses, says, "I honored my father, I esteemed my mother, I loved my brothers. I found graves for the unburied dead. I instructed little children. I took care of orphans as though they were my own children. For great misfortunes were on Egypt in my time, and on this city of Sais."

In speaking of the ancient books of Egyptian wisdom - the "Ptah-Hotep" and the "Ke- Gemni," Dr. Battiscombe Gunn says: "Nor do the oldest books of any other country approach these two in antiquity. To draw comparisons between them let us, in imagination, place ourselves at the period at which Ptah-hotep lived, that is, about B.C. 3550, under King Isôsi, and take a glance at futurity.

"The Babylonians are doubtless exercising their literary talents; but they will leave nothing worthy the name of book to the far posterity of fifty-four centuries hence. Thirteen centuries shall pass before Hammurabi, king of Babylon, drafts the code of laws that will be found at that time. Only after two thousand years shall Moses write on the origin of things, and the Vedas be arranged in their present form. It will be two-and-a-half thousand years before the great king of Jerusalem will set in order many proverbs and write books so much resembling, in form and style, that of Ptahhotep; before the source and summit of European literature will write his world epics. For the space of years between Solomon and ourselves, great though it seem, is not so great as that between Solomon and Ptah-hotep."

Dr. Wallis Budge sums up the Egyptian character thus: "A good general idea of the average Egyptian can be derived from the monuments and writings that have come down to us. In the first place he was a very religious man. He worshipped God and his deified ancestors, offered sacrifices and offerings to the dead, and prayed at least twice daily, i.e., morning and evening. He believed in the resurrection of the dead through Osiris, and in the life everlasting, and was from first to last confident that those who had led righteous lives on earth were rewarded with happiness and lived with Osiris in heaven, and that the wicked on earth were punished with annihilation in the next world. His deep-seated interest in religion had a very practical object, namely, the resurrection of his spirit-body and his soul's future happiness in heaven. His conscience was well developed and made him obey religious, moral, and civil laws without question; a breach of any of these he atoned for, not by repentance, for which there is no word in his language, but by the making of offerings. In all religious matters he was strongly conservative, and his conservatism led him to hold at the same time beliefs that were not only inconsistent with each other, but sometimes flatly contradictory. In reality his religious books are filled with obsolete beliefs, many of which were contradicted by his religious observances. He had a keen sense of humor and was easily pleased. He loved eating and drinking, music and dancing, festivals and processions, and display of all sorts and kinds, and he enjoyed himself whenever an opportunity offered. Over and over again the living are exhorted to eat and drink and enjoy themselves. His morality was of the highest kind, and he thoroughly understood his duty towards his neighbor. He was kindly and humane, he fed the hungry, gave drink to the thirsty, lent a boat to the shipwrecked man, protected the widows and orphans, and fed the starving animals of the desert. He loved his village and his home and rejoiced when he was 'loved by his father, praised by his mother, and beloved by his brothers and sisters.' He was a hard worker, as the taxes wrung from him by tax-gatherers and priests in all periods testify. He was intensely superstitious, and was easily duped by the magician and medicine man, who provided him with spells and incantations and amulets of all kinds. He was slow to anger and disliked military service and war. His idea of heaven was the possession of a homestead in a fertile district, with streams of water and luxuriant crops of wheat, barley, fruit, etc., wherein he would live a life of leisure surrounded by all those whom he had known and loved upon earth. He had no wish to enlarge the borders of Egypt, except for the loot which raids brought in; he never sought to bestow the blessings of Egyptian civilization upon other lands, and he never indulged in missionary enterprises of any kind. His religious toleration was great. He was content to serve God and Pharaoh, and he wished above all things to be allowed to till his land and do his own business in his own way in peace.

"The influence of his beliefs and religion, and literature, and arts and crafts on the civilization of other nations can hardly be overestimated. In one of the least known periods of the world's history he proclaimed the deathlessness of the human soul, and his country has rightly been named the 'land of immortality.'"

CHAPTER I

THE STORY OF EGYPT

Egypt has been called the "Father of History and the Mother of Civilization" and well may she be called both for her influence upon the ancient world must have been great. Thales, the founder of Greek philosophy, was a student of Egyptian thought and investigated all of their theories of the universe as well as their ideas about the gods. Herodotus, a Greek historian who visited Egypt about 450 B.C., has given a vivid description of the country and people, at that time and about 8 B.C. Diodorus Siculus, a Greek traveler, wandered up and down the bank of the Nile and he, like Herodotus, gives in his book a description of the country and the people. By far the most interesting, as well as accurate, account is given by Strabo, the great geographer of Greece, who was a contemporary of Diodorus. About 90 A.D., Plutarch wrote his celebrated treatise on Isis and Osiris, a work that Egyptologists today consider a most accurate presentation of the ideals and traditions of ancient Egypt.

In speaking of the sources for the historical material pertaining to the ancient Egyptian, Auguste Mariette in his short history said: "First and foremost in value and in quantity are the Egyptian monuments themselves: the temples, palaces, tombs, statues, and inscriptions. These have supreme authority, because they have the advantage of being the incontestable evidence of the events which they record. They have not long enjoyed this distinction, as the secret of the mysterious writing with which they are covered was, until lately, lost; and it was difficult to see in these relies of antiquity anything more than lifeless stones, devoid of interest. But about eighty-five years ago there appeared, in the person of Champollion, a true genius, who succeeded, by his keen insight, in throwing the most unexpected light upon the darkness of the Egyptian script. Through him these old monuments, so long silent, caused their voices to be heard; by him was the veil torn asunder, and the Egypt of bygone days, so renowned for her wisdom and power, stood revealed to the modern world.

No longer are the monuments objects of hopeless curiosity, rather are they books of stone wherein may be read, in legible writing, the history of the nation with which they were contemporaneous.

"Next to the monuments in importance comes the Greek history of Egypt, written by Manetho, an Egyptian priest, about B.C. 250; and were the book itself in existence, we could have no more trustworthy guide. Egyptian by birth and priest by profession, Manetho, besides being instructed in all the mysteries of his religion, must have also been conversant with foreign literature, for he was a Greek scholar, and equal to the task of writing a complete history of his own country in that language. If only we had that book today it would be a priceless treasure; but the work of the Egyptian priest perished, along with many others, in the great wreck of ancient literature, the burning of the great library at

Alexandria, and all we possess of it are a few fragments preserved in the pages of subsequent historians."

ORIGIN OF THE EGYPTIAN RACE

Prof. Wallis Budge writes on the Egyptian race: "The flint tools and weapons that have been found on the skirts of the desert at various places in Egypt, and that are generally admitted to be older than those of the Neolithic period, i.e., the New Stone Age, render it extremely probable that the country was inhabited by men in the Palæolithic period, i.e., the Old Stone Age. The questions that naturally arise in connection with them are: Who were they? To what race did they belong? If they were immigrants, where did they come from? In the limited space afforded by a single chapter it is impossible to enumerate even the most important of the arguments of which these questions have formed the subjects, or the principal theories, old and new, of the origin of the Egyptians. Fortunately Egyptian archæology, even in its present imperfect state, supplies a number of facts, which will suggest answers to these questions that are tolerably correct; and, as time goes on and the results of further research are perfected, our knowledge of these difficult questions may assume a decisive character. The human remains that have been found in Neolithic graves in Egypt prove that the Egyptians of the Neolithic period in upper Egypt were Africans, and there is good reason for thinking that they were akin to all the other inhabitants of the Nile Valley at that time. When the great geological change took place that turned into a river valley the arm of the sea that extended as far as Esnâ, and the Nile deposits had formed the soil of Egypt, their ancestors migrated from the south to the north and occupied the land made by the Nile. Whether these facts apply equally to the Delta cannot be said, for no Neolithic graves in the Delta are known. Egyptian tradition of the Dynastic period held that the aboriginal home of the Egyptians was Punt, and though our information about the boundaries of this land is of the vaguest character, it is quite certain that a very large portion of it was in central Africa, and it probably was near the country called in our times 'Uganda.' There was in all periods frequent intercourse between Egypt and Punt, and caravans must have journeyed from one country to the other at least once a year. In the dynastic period several missions by sea were despatched to the port of Punt to bring back myrrh and other products of the country, which were so dear to the heart of the kinsmen of the Puntites who were settled in Egypt.

"Now, if the inhabitants of the southern portion of the Valley of the Nile were attracted to the good and fertile land of Egypt, it follows, as a matter of course, that foreign peoples who heard of this rich land would migrate thither in order to partake of its products and to settle in it. The peoples on the western bank - Libyans - and the dwellers in the eastern desert would intermarry with the native Egyptians, and the same would be the case with the negro and half-negro tribes in the Sûdân. At a very early period, and certainly in Neolithic times, a considerable number of Semites must have made their way into Egypt, and these came from the Arabian peninsula on the other side of the Red Sea, either for trading purposes or to settle in Egypt. Some of these crossed the Red Sea in its narrowest part, probably near the straits of Bâb al- Mandib at the southern end of it, and made their way into the country where the comparatively modern town of Sennaar now stands, just as their descendants did some three to five thousand years later. Here they would find themselves not only in fertile land, but they would also be in touch with the tribes living in the region where, from time immemorial, alluvial gold has been found in considerable quantities. Others of the Semites must have made their way into the Delta by the Isthmus of Suez, and there is no doubt that by intermarriage they modified the physical characteristics of many of the natives. Others, again, must have entered Egypt by way of the very ancient caravan route through the Wadi Hammânât, which left the Red Sea near the modern town of Kusêr and ended on the Nile near Kenâ in upper Egypt. It is impossible to think that the Semites in Arabia had no seagoing boats in which to cross the Red Sea, and that those who lived on the coast halfway down the Red Sea would be obliged to go so far north as the Isthmus of Suez, or so far south as Bâb al-Mandib before they could cross over into Africa.

"In the case of the natives of the Delta foreign influences of another kind would be at work. Here would flock traders of all kinds from the land that is now called Palestine, and from the islands of the Mediterranean, and from the seacoast and the countries inland to the west of Egypt. Some think that even in the Neolithic period there were many settlers who had come from the southern countries of Europe. If the above remarks are only approximately true, we are justified in assuming that the population of the Valley of the Nile was even at this early period very much mixed. It must, however, be noted that neither Libyans, nor Semites, nor seafaring folk of any kind, altered the fundamental characteristics of the African dwellers on the Nile."

THE BEGINNING OF EGYPTIAN HISTORY

Towards the end of the New Stone Age the Egyptians acquired the knowledge of working in copper, and with tools of this metal they found themselves able to do many things that were before impossible to them. With copper drills they perforated beads and hollowed out stone jars and vessels, and with copper knives and chisels they sculptured stone figures of men, animals, etc., with a skill that was truly wonderful. They had long known how to produce fire and one of its principal uses among them was to smelt copper. In many respects the state of Egypt at the close of this period was not greatly unlike that in which we know it to have been in the earliest part of the dynastic period. It was divided roughly into districts, or as we might say, counties, which at a later period were called "nomes" by the Greeks. Each district had its own symbol, which was generally that of its totem, and probably its own god, or gods, who must have been served by some kind of priest. The laws which men draw up for the protection of their wives, cattle, and possessions generally, as soon as they settle down in towns and villages, were, no doubt, administered in the rough and ready way that has been common among African communities from time immemorial. A system of irrigation must have been in use at this time, but it is improbable that there was any central controlling authority. The men of each district protected the part of the bank of the Nile that belonged to them, and made and maintained their own canals, and the high, banked causeways, which connected the towns and villages during the period of the Nile flood, and served as roads. There must have been a head man or governor in each district who possessed a good deal of power, and each town was probably ruled by a kind of mayor with due regard to the interests of the owners of large properties of different kinds. In the villages the largest landowners were probably supreme, but the "old men" or "fathers" of each village must have enjoyed a certain authority.

For a considerable time before the dynastic period there must have been kings in Egypt, some ruling over upper Egypt, and some over lower Egypt and the Delta. A portion of a monument, now called the "Palermo Stone" because it is preserved in the museum of Palermo in Sicily, supplies the names of several kings of lower Egypt, e.g., Seka, Tau, Thesh, Neheb, Uatchnâr, and Mekha. It is quite certain that the names of several kings of upper Egypt were given on the missing portion of the monument, and this fact proves that at that time southern and northern Egypt formed two separate and independent kingdoms. When complete the Palermo stone contained a series of annals, which recorded the principal events in the reigns of the pre-dynastic kings, and also of the dynastic kings down to the middle of the fifth dynasty. There were also included the names of the principal festivals that were celebrated in these reigns, and also the height of the Nile flood yearly, given in cubits, palms, fingers, and spans. How these heights were ascertained is not clear, but it was probably by means of lines cut into a rock on the river bank, or on a slab built into a wall of a well at Memphis. The height of the Nile flood then, as now, was valuable for determining the degree of prosperity of the country that was probable during the year.

We have already said that the native African element in upper Egypt was reinforced continually from the south, and we may assume that the process of reinforcement usually went on peacefully, and that the Egyptians in upper Egypt assimilated their newly-arrived kinsmen from the south without difficulty. This, however, was fated not to go on indefinitely, for on one occasion at least, probably a century or two before the dynastic period began, a host of men from the south or southeast swept down upon Egypt. This invasion in many respects seems to have been similar to that which took place under Piânkhi, the king of Nubia, whose capital was at Napt, or Napata, about 720 B.C.; but whilst Piânkhi returned to Nubia, the southern folk and their leaders who invaded Egypt towards the close of the pre-dynastic period did not do so. If we take into account the effect of this pre-dynastic invasion upon the civilization of Egypt we must assume that the invaders were more highly civilized than the people they conquered. And if we assume this we must further assume that the invaders came from the country now called Abyssinia and the lands to the south of it. Their route was the old trade route known today as the "Blue Nile caravan route," which has been chosen from time immemorial by the captains of caravans, because it makes it unnecessary to traverse the first four cataracts. Among the invaders who came by this route were natives of the Eastern Desert, the remote ancestors of the Blemmyes and the modern Hadenduwa and cognate tribes, and Semites, who had originally crossed the Red Sea from Asia to Africa. We have no distinct record of this invasion, still less have we any details of it, and we have no knowledge of the causes that led up to it; but in an inscription of the Ptolemaic period cut on the walls of the temple of Edfû in upper Egypt, we certainly have a legendary account of it. In this inscription the victorious leader is accompanied by men who are called "Mesniu," or "Blacksmiths," who came from the west of the Nile, i.e., from a country to the south of Egypt, and not from a country to the southeast. This view agrees quite well with what is known of the dynastic period, for the Pharaohs often had to fight hordes of enemies from countries so far south as the White Nile and the Gazelle and Jûr Rivers, and their descendants were probably to be found in the Nobadae, who terrified the Romans, and the "Baggârah" who fought under the Mahdi in our own times. There may have been a conquest of Egypt by the peoples to the west of Egypt at one time, and another by the peoples to the east at another time, or the enemies of Egypt on both banks of the White and Blue Niles may have invaded the country together. In any case the purport of the inscription, the contents of which we will now describe, is to show that the king of the south and his descendants first conquered upper Egypt and then lower Egypt.

The Edfu text sets forth that Râ-Harmakhis was king of Ta-sti, the "Land of the Bow," i.e., the country of all the peoples who fought with bows and arrows, or the eastern Sûdân. In the 363d year of his reign he dispatched a force into Egypt, and overcoming all opposition, this god established himself and his followers at Edfû. Having discovered that the enemy had collected in force to the southeast of Thebes, Horus and his followers, or the blacksmiths, armed with spears and chains, set out and joined battle with them, and utterly defeated them at a place called Tchetmet. For the first time probably the natives armed with weapons made of flint found themselves in mortal combat with foreign enemies armed with metal weapons; their defeat was unavoidable. Soon after this battle the natives again collected in force to the northeast of Denderah, about fifty miles north of Thebes, where they were attacked and again defeated by Horus. Another battle took place a little later on at Heben, about one hundred and fifty miles south of Memphis, and Horus cut up many of his defeated foes and offered them to the gods. Horus then pursued the enemy into the Delta, and wherever he did battle with them he defeated them.

In one place the arch-rebel Set appeared with his followers and fought against Horus and his "blacksmiths," but Horus drove his spear into Set's neck, fettered his limbs with his chain, and then cut off his head, and the heads of all his followers. Horus then sailed over the streams in the Delta, and slew the enemy in detail, and made himself master of the whole of the Delta, from the swamps on the west of the left main arm of the Nile to the desert in the east. The text goes on to say that companies of the "blacksmiths" settled down on lands given to them by Horus on the right and left banks of the Nile and in what is now called "middle Egypt"; thus the followers of Horus from the south effectively occupied the country. Horus returned to Edfû and made an expedition against the people of Uauat (now northern Nubia), and punished their rebellion. He then sailed back to Edfû and established the worship of Horus of Edfû, and ordered a symbol of this god to be placed in every temple of Egypt. Now the symbol referred to is the winged solar disk, with a serpent on each side of it, and the statement suggests that Horus established the worship of a form of the sun-god in Egypt. If this be really so, Horus and his followers must have come from the east, where sun-worship was common, and must have found that the Egyptians were not sun-worshippers. The Egyptians, like most of the peoples in the Nile Valley, ancient and modem, only worshipped the sun under compulsion. On the other hand, the worship of the moon was universal, and the native gods of the Egyptians were of a kind quite different from those worshipped in the Eastern Desert and among the peoples of Arabia, Syria, and the northern Delta.

BEGINNING OF DYNASTIC HISTORY

As the result, however, of one of the battles between the forces of the south and north, which was fought probably near Anulater Heliopolis - the king of the south gained the victory, and he was henceforth able to call himself "King of the South, King of the North." Who this mighty "uniter of the two lands" really was is not known, but the native tradition, which was current at Abydos, and presumably throughout Egypt, in the thirteenth century before Christ, stated that he was called Mena; this tradition was also accepted in the time of the Greek historians, for they all agree in saying that the first king of Egypt was called Menes.

MANETHO - THE EGYPTIAN HISTORIAN ON THE DYNASTIES

In this history of Egypt, Manetho gave a list of the kings of Egypt, which he divided into three parts, each containing several groups of kings which he called "dynasties," but it is not quite clear what he meant by the word "dynasty." Though his history is lost, four copies of his king-list are preserved in the works of later writers. The oldest of these is that which is said to have been written by Julius Africanus, in the third century of our era, which is preserved in the "Chronicle of Eusebius," bishop of Cæsarea, born A.D. 264, and died about 340. In this work Eusebius also gives a copy of the list of Manetho made by himself, but the copy of Julius Africanus agrees better with the results derived from the monuments which we now have than that of Eusebius. The dynasties of Manetho's king-list that represent that "archaic period" are the first three. According to this, the kings of the first dynasty were eight in number and reigned 263 years; those of the second dynasty were nine in number and reigned 214 years. The first and second dynasties reigned at Thnis - Abydos - and the third dynasty at Memphis. The original Egyptian forms of many of the royal names given by Manetho have been identified without doubt; the identifications of a few others are nearly certain, and about the remainder there exist many different opinions. Besides Áha and Nârmer, or Nârmer and Áha, for the true order of these two kings is uncertain.

THE DYNASTIES OF ANCIENT EGYPT

Dynasties		Duration in years
ANCIENT EMPIRE		
1-2	Thinite	555
3-5	Memphite	746
6	Elephantine	203
7-8	Memphite	142 years, 70 days
9-10	Heracleopolite	294
MIDDLE EMPIRE		
11-13	Theban	666
14	Xoite	184
15-17	Hyksos (Delta)	511
NEW EMPIRE		
18-20	Theban	593
21	Tanite	130
22	Bubastite	170
23	Tanite	89
24	Saïte	6
25	Ethiopian	50
26	Saïte	138
27	Persian	121
28	Saïte	7
29	Mendesian	21

30	Sebennyte	38
31	Persian	8

PRINCIPAL KINGS

Dynasties	Kings
1	Mena
	Teta
	Hesepti
2	Ba-en-neter
3	Sneferu
4	Khufu
	Khafra
	Menkau-Ra
5	Unas
6	Teta
	Pepi I
	Pepi II
	Queen Nitocris
12	Amen-em-hat I
	Usertsen I
	Amen-em-hat II
	Usertsen II
	Usertsen III
	Amen-em-hat III
	Amen-em-hat IV
17	Sekenen-Ra
18	Aahmes I
	Amen-hotep I
	Thothmes II
	Queen Hatshepsu
	Thothmes III
	Amen-hotep II
	Thothmes IV
	Amen-hotep III
	Amen-hotep IV
	Akhnaton
	Semenkhkara - or Saakara
	Tutankhaton -
	after Tutankhamon

Dynasties	Kings
19	Seti I
	Ramses II
	Merenptah
20	Ramses III
21	Her-Hor
22	Shashanq I (Shishak)
	Osorkon II (Zerah?)
23	Tefnekht (Piankhi King of Ethiopia took Memphis)
	Bakenranef (Bocchoris)
25	Shabaka. His sister Ameniritis married Piankhi II and their daughter became the queen of Psamethek I
	Shabataka
26	Taharaqa (Tirhakah)
	Psamethe I
	Neku II (Necho)
30	Uahabra (Hophra)
	Nekthorheb (Nectanebo I)
	Nektnebef (Nectanebo II)

THOTHMES III OF THE EIGHTEENTH DYNASTY

Thothmes III is generally regarded as the greatest of the kings of Egypt - the Alexander the Great of the Egyptian history. The name Thothmes means "child of Thoth," and was a common name among the ancient Egyptians. He is represented by a sphinx presenting gifts of water and wine to Tum, the setting sun, a solar deity worshipped at Heliopolis. On the hieroglyphic paintings at Karnak, the fact of the heliacal rising of Sothis, the dog-star, is stated to have taken place during this reign, from which it appears that Thothmes III occupied the throne of Egypt about 1450 B.C. This is one of the few dates of Egyptian chronology that can be authenticated.

Thothmes III belonged to the eighteenth dynasty, which included some of the greatest of Egyptian monarchs. Among the kings of this dynasty were four that bore the name of Thothmes, and four the name of Amenophis, which means "peace of Amen." The monarchs of this dynasty were Thebans.

The father of Thothmes III was a great warrior. He conquered the Canaanitish nations of Palestine, took Nineveh from the Rutennu, the confederate tribes of Syria, laid waste Mesopotamia, and introduced war chariots and horses into the army of Egypt.

18

Thothmes III, however, was even a greater warrior than his father; and during his long reign Egypt reached the climax of her greatness. His predecessors of the eighteenth dynasty had extended the dominions of Egypt far into Asia and the interior of Africa. He was a king of great capacity and a warrior of considerable courage. The records of his campaigns are for the most part preserved on a sandstone wall surrounding the great temple of Karnak, built by Thothmes III in honor of Amen-Ra. From these hieroglyphic inscriptions it appears that Thothmes' first great campaign was made in the twenty-second year of his reign, when an expedition was made into the land of Taneter, that is, Palestine. A full account of his marches and victories is given, together with a list of one hundred and nineteen conquered towns.

This monarch lived before the time of Joshua, and therefore the records of his conquests present us with the ancient Canaanite nomenclature of places in Palestine between the times of the patriarchs and the conquest of the land by the Israelites under Joshua. Thothmes set out with his army from Tanis, that is Zoan; and after taking Gaza, he proceeded, by way of the plain of Sharon, to the more northern parts of Palestine. At the battle of Megiddo he overthrew the confederated troops of native princes; and in consequence of this signal victory the whole of Palestine was subdued. Crossing the Jordan near the Sea of Galilee, Thothmes pursued his march to Damascus, which he took by the sword; and then returning homeward by the Judean hills and the south country of Palestine, he returned to Egypt laden with the spoils of victory.

In the thirtieth year of his reign Thothmes led an expedition against the Rutennu, the people of northern Syria. In this campaign he attacked and captured Kadesh, a strong fortress in the valley of Orontes, and the capital town of the Rutennu. The king pushed his conquests into Mesopotamia, and occupied the strong fortress of Carchemish, on the banks of the Euphrates. He then led his conquering troops northward to the sources of the Tigris and the Euphrates, so that the kings of Damascus, Nineveh, and Assur became his vassals, and paid tribute to Egypt.

Punt or Arabia was also subdued, and in Africa his conquests extended to Cush or Ethiopia. His fleet of ships sailed triumphantly over the waters of the Black Sea. Thus Thothmes ruled over lands extending from the mountains of Caucasus to the shores of the Indian Ocean, and from the Libyan Desert to the great river Tigris.

Besides distinguishing himself as a warrior and as a record writer, Thothmes III was one of the greatest of Egyptian builders and patrons of art. The great temple of Ammon at Thebes was the special object of his fostering care, and he began his career of builder and restorer by repairing the damages which his sister Hatasu had inflicted on that glorious edifice to gratify her dislike of her brother Thothmes III, and her father Thothmes I, Statues of Thothmes I and his father Amenophis, which Hatasu had thrown down, were re-erected by Thothmes III, before the southern propylæa of the temple in the first year of his independent reign. The central sanctuary which Usertesen I had built in common stone, was next replaced by the present granite edifice, under the directions of the young prince, who then proceeded to build in the rear of the old temple a magnificent hall or pillared chamber of dimensions previously unknown in Egypt. This edifice was an oblong square, one hundred and forty-three feet long by fifty-five feet wide, or nearly half as large again as our largest cathedral. The whole of this apartment was roofed in with slabs of solid stone; two rows of circular pillars thirty feet in height supported the central part, dividing it into three avenues, while on each side of the pillars was a row of square piers, still further extending the width of the chamber and breaking it up into five long vistas. In connection with this noble ball, on three sides of it, north, east, and south, Thothmes erected further chambers and corridors, one of the former situated towards the south containing the "Great Table of Karnak."

One of the most interesting Pharaohs of Egypt was Akhnaton, who is called the first individualist of history and a great idealist. Prof. Wallis Budge gives this account of his kingship:

"Amen-Hetep - Akhnaton - was the son of Amen-hetep III by his wife Tî, and he reigned about twenty years. Whether he ascended the throne immediately after his father's death is not known, but whether he did or not matters little, for it is quite certain that for some years at least his mother was the actual ruler of Egypt, and that she ordered works to be carried out as if she were its lawful sovereign. His wife Nefertithi, who was probably of Asiatic origin like his mother, also obtained a power and an authority in Egypt which were not usually enjoyed by Egyptian queens. These facts are proved by the monuments, in which both Tî and Nefertithi are represented as equals in every respect of Amen-hetep IV, and their names are accorded prominence similar to those of the king. The pictures and sculptured representations of Amen-hetep IV show that his physical characteristics were wholly of a non-Egyptian character, and suggest that he was of a highly nervous and sensitive disposition, lacking in purpose, firmness, and decision, full of prejudices, self-will, and obstinacy. His acts prove that he was unpractical in every matter connected with the rule of Egypt and her Nubian and Asiatic provinces, which had been won for her by the great Thothmes III, and the story of the break-up of the great Egyptian empire owing to his weakness and incapacity is almost the saddest page of Egyptian history. His alien blood, derived from his mother and grandmother, caused to develop in him a multitude of strange ideas about religion, art, and government that were detestable to the Egyptians, whose national characteristics he neither recognized nor understood, and with whom he had no true sympathy. When he ascended the throne he adopted a series of names that proclaimed to all Egypt that he held religious views of a different character from those held by the majority of the Egyptians. Some of these resembled the doctrines of the Sun-god as taught by the priests of

Heliopolis, but others were obnoxious to the Egyptians generally. His father and grandfather probably held exactly the same religious views, but if they did they took care not to allow them to disturb the peace of the country, nor to interrupt the business of the state. Amen-hetep IV proclaimed a new form of worship, and, to all intents and purposes, a new god, whom he called Aten. Now Aten was well known to the Egyptians as the god of the solar disk, and they had been familiar with him from the earliest period; but Amen-hetep IV assigned to him new attributes, which are very difficult to describe. He taught that Aten was the unseen, almighty, and everlasting power that made itself manifest in the form of the solar disk in the sky, and was the source of all life in heaven and earth and the underworld. He ascribed to Aten a monotheistic character, or oneness, which he denied to every other god, but when we read the hymns to Aten of which the king approved, it is extremely difficult to understand the difference between the oneness of Aten and the oneness of Amen-Râ, or Râ, or of any other great Egyptian god.

"During the first four years of his reign Amen-hetep IV lived at Thebes, but during the whole of this period he was quarrelling actively with the priests of Amen-Râ, whose god Amen was an abomination to him. As king he had great resources at his command, and besides building a sanctuary called Kem Aten at Thebes, he set up shrines to Aten at various places in Egypt, and also in the Sudan. The most important in the latter country was Kem Aten, which was probably situated at or near Sadengah, where his father had built a temple in honor of Queen Tî. Whilst this work was going on Amen-hetep IV caused the name of Amen to be hammered out from the inscriptions on existing monuments, and he suppressed by every means in his power the cults of the other gods. Such an intolerant religious fanatic was never before seen in Egypt, and the king hated Amen and his name so thoroughly that he changed his own name from Amen-hetep to "Khu-en-Aten," or "Aakh-en-Aten," a name meaning "spirit soul of Aten." Besides his fanaticism there was also a material reason for his hatred of Amen. He saw the greater part of the revenues of the country being absorbed slowly but surely by the greedy priesthood of this god, and he felt that their wealth made their power to be actually greater than that of the king.

"Of the details of the fight between the priesthoods of the old gods of Egypt and the king little is known, but it is clear that the Egyptians found some effective way of showing their resentment to the king, for in the fifth year of his reign he forsook Thebes, and founded a new capital, wherein Aten alone was to be worshipped. The site of the new capital which was called Khut-en-Aten, or 'horizon of Aten,' was on the east bank of the Nile, about two hundred miles south of Memphis, and is marked today by the villages of Haggî Kandil, and Tell al-Amarnah. Here he built a large temple to Aten and two or three smaller sanctuaries for the private use of the ladies of his family. Near the temple was the palace, which was splendidly decorated and furnished with beautiful objects of every kind, and the priests and high officials and nobles who had followed the king were provided with rock-hewn tombs in the mountain behind the new capital. A considerable space of ground about this capital was set apart as the property of Aten, and its confines were marked with boundary stones, and the revenues of some of the old sanctuaries were wrested from them by the king and applied to the support of Aten. Amen-hetep IV and his followers lived in Khut-en-Aten for some twelve or fifteen years in comparative peace, and the king occupied himself in playing the priest, and in superintending the building operations and the laying out of large and beautiful gardens by the court architect Bek. The high priest bore the title of the high priest of Heliopolis, and the form of worship there seems to have had much in common with the old solar cult of Heliopolis. The king composed one or two hymns which were sung in his temple, and copies of these were painted on the walls of the tombs of his favourites.

"Meanwhile what was happening to Egypt and her Asiatic and Nubian provinces? For a time the kings of Mitanni and Babylonia sent dispatches to Amen-hetep IV as they did to his father, and some of the chiefs of the neighboring countries sent tribute to him as they did to his father. When, however, the envoys returned to their countries and reported that Pharaoh, whose mere name had struck terror into the Asiatics, was at enmity with all his people, and was devoting all his time to theological matters, and to the founding of new canons of art, and to the selfish enjoyment of a religion that was detested by all the Egyptian priesthoods, with the exception of the priesthood of Heliopolis, the enemies of the Egyptian power in western Asia felt that the time of their deliverance was at hand. With one accord they ceased to pay tribute, and gathering together their forces, they attacked the Egyptian garrisons in Syria and Palestine, and one by one the cities fell, and the Egyptian governors and their troops were slain or scattered. The Kheta, or Hittites, swept down from the north upon the possessions of Egypt, and being joined by the Khabiri and by the vassal princes of Egypt, were irresistible. They first attacked and took the inland cities, and then advancing westward they captured city after city along the coast until Beyrut, Tyre, Ascalon, Gezer, and Lachish were at their mercy. The Tell al-Amarnah letters contain piteous appeals to Amen-hetep IV for help from all parts of Syria and Palestine, and every writer entreats the king to protect his own possessions; but the king had no help to send, and even if he had had troops available for despatch they would never have been sent, for he hated war in all its forms. Thus Egypt lost her Asiatic possessions which it had taken her kings nearly two hundred years to acquire. Meanwhile discontent was growing everywhere in Egypt itself, and conspiracies against the king were spreading in all directions; when these had reached formidable proportions the king died, but whether his death was due to anxiety, disease, or poison cannot be said. Amen-hetep IV had no son, and his family consisted of six daughters, the eldest of whom died before her father. He was buried in a tomb hewn in the mountains behind his town, and his stone coffin, or sarcophagus, was found there in 1893 by the native tomb robbers, who cut out the cartouches from it and sold them to travellers.

"Amen-hetep IV was succeeded by Sâakarâ who had married one of his daughters called Merit-Aten, and had probably assisted his father-in-law in his various religious undertakings. Sâakarâ ruled the town of Khut-en-Aten for two or three years, and was succeeded by Tut-Ánkh-Amen, a son of Amen-hetep III, who married a daughter of Amen-hetep IV called Ánkhsenpaaten. Tut-ânkh-Amen was undoubtedly supported by the priests of Amen, as the presence of the name of the god in his name testifies, and his accession to the throne marks the triumph of the priesthood of Amen over Aten and his followers. He made his wife change her name to Ankhsen-Amen, and removed the court to Thebes, where he at once set to work to repair portions of the great temples of Amen at Karnak and Luxor. Wherever it was possible to do so he restored the name and figure of the god Amen, which his father-in-law had attempted to obliterate. He carried out certain building operations in the Sudan and received tribute from the chiefs of the country, but he undertook no military expeditions into Syria, and made no attempt to renew the sovereignty of Egypt in western Asia. When Tut-Ankh-Amen removed his court to Thebes, he was quickly followed by many of the nobles who had settled at Khut-en-Aten, and the capital of Amen-hetep IV began at once to decline. The services in the temple languished, and the sculptors and artists who had designed their works in accordance with the canons of art devised and approved by Amen-hetep IV found themselves without employment; the working classes who had lived on the court left the town, which in a very few years became forsaken. The Aten temples were thrown down, and before many years had passed the town became a heap of ruins. Thus the triumph of Amen, the god who had delivered the Egyptians from the Nyksos, was complete."

RAMESES II OF THE NINETEENTH DYNASTY

Rameses II, called the Napoleon of Egypt, lived about two centuries after Thothmes III, and ascended the throne about 1300 B.C. Rameses I was the third king of the nineteenth dynasty; and for personal exploits, the magnificence of his works, and the length of his reign, he was not surpassed by any of the kings of ancient Egypt, except by Thothmes III.

His grandfather, Rameses I, was the founder of the dynasty. His father, Seti I, is celebrated for his victories over the Rutennu, or Syrians, and over the Shasu, or Arabians, as well as for his public works, especially the great temple he built at Karnak. Rameses II, was, however, a greater warrior than his father. He first conquered Kush, or Ethiopia; then he led an expedition against the Khitæ, or Hittites, whom he completely routed at Kadesh, the ancient capital, a town on the River Orontes, north of Mount Lebanon. In this battle Rameses was placed. in the greatest danger; but his personal bravery stood him in good stead, and he kept the Hittites at bay till his soldiers rescued him. He thus commemorates on the monuments his deeds:

"I became like the god Mentu; I hurled the dart with my right hand; I fought with my left hand; I was like Baal in his time before their slight; I had come upon two thousand five hundred pairs of horses; I was in the midst of them; but they were dashed in pieces before my steeds. Not one of them raised his hand to fight; their courage was sunken in their breasts; their limbs gave way; they could not hurl the dart, nor had they strength to thrust the spear. I made them fall into the waters like crocodiles; they tumbled down on their faces one after another. I killed them at my pleasure, so that not one looked back behind him; nor did any turn round. Each fell, and none raised himself up again."[1]

Rameses fought with and conquered the Amorites, Canaanites, and other tribes of Palestine and Syria. His public works are also very numerous; he dug wells, founded cities, and completed a great wall begun by his father Seti, reaching from Pelusium to Heliopolis, a gigantic structure designed to keep back the hostile Asiatics, thus reminding one of the Great Wall of China. Pelusium was situated near the present Port Said, and the wall must therefore have been about a hundred miles long. In its course it must have passed near the site of Tel-el-Kebir. It is now certain that Rameses built the treasure cities spoken of in Exodus: "Therefore they did set over them taskmasters to afflict them with their burdens. And they built for Pharaoh treasure cities, Pithom and Raamses" - Exod. i. 11. According to Dr. Brich, Rameses II was a monarch of whom it was written: "Now there arose up a new king over Egypt who knew not Joseph."

He enlarged On and Tanis, and built temples at Ipsambul, Karnak, Luxor, Abydos, Memphis, etc.

The most remarkable of the temples erected by Rameses is the building at Thebes, once called the Memnonium, but now commonly known as the Rameseum; and the extraordinary rock temple of Ipsambul, or Abu-Simbel, the most magnificent specimen of its class which the world contains.

The façade is formed by four huge colossi, each seventy feet in height, representing Rameses himself seated on a throne, with the double crown of Egypt upon his head. In the center, flanked on either side by two of these gigantic figures, is a doorway of the usual Egyptian type, opening into a small vestibule, which communicates by a short passage with the main chamber. This is an oblong square, sixty feet long, by forty-five, divided into a nave and two aisles by two rows of square piers with Osirid statues, thirty feet high in front, and ornamented with painted sculptures over its whole surface. The main chamber leads into an inner shrine or adytum, supported by four piers with Osirid figures, but otherwise as richly adorned as the outer apartment. Behind the adytum. are small rooms for the priests who served in the temple. It is the façade of the work which constitutes its main beauty." [2]

"The largest of the rock temples at Ipsambul," says Mr. Fergusson, "is the finest of its class known to exist anywhere. Externally the façade is about one hundred feet in height, and adorned by four of the most magnificent colossi in Egypt, each seventy feet in height, and representing the king, Rameses II, who caused the excavation to be made."

His character has been well summarized by Canon Rawlinson: "His affection for his son, and for his two principal wives, shows that the disposition of Rameses II was in some respects amiable; although, upon the whole, his character is one which scarcely commends itself to our approval. Professing in his early years extreme devotion to the memory of his father, he lived to show himself his father's worst enemy, and to aim at obliterating his memory by erasing his name from the monuments on which it occurred, and in many cases substituting his own. Amid a great show of regard for the deities of his country, and for the ordinances of the established worship, he contrived that the chief result of all that he did for religion should be the glorification of himself. Other kings had arrogated to themselves a certain qualified dignity, and after their deaths had sometimes been placed by some of their successors on a par with the real national gods; but it remained for Rameses to associate himself during his lifetime with such leading deities as Ptah, Ammon, and Horus, and to claim equally with them the religious regards of his subjects. He was also, as already observed, the first to introduce into Egypt the degrading custom of polygamy and the corrupting influence of a harem. Even his bravery, which cannot be denied, loses half its merit by being made the constant subject of boasting; and his magnificence ceases to appear admirable when we think at what a cost it displayed itself. If, with most recent writers upon Egyptian history, we identify him with the 'king who knew not Joseph,' the builder of Pithom and Raamses, the first oppressor of the Israelites, we must add some darker shades to the picture, and look upon him as a cruel and ruthless despot, who did not shrink from inflicting on innocent persons the severest pain and suffering."

Footnotes
1. Brugsch, "History of Egypt," Vol. II, p. 5U, 1st ed.
2. Rawlinson's "Ancient Egypt," Vol. I, p. 318.

CHAPTER II
RELIGION OF ANCIENT EGYPT

EGYPTIAN VIEW OF CREATION

Man in all times and places, has speculated on the nature and origin of the world, and connected such questions with his theology. In Egypt there are not many primitive theories of creation, though some have various elaborated forms. Of the formation of the earth there were two views.

(1) That it had been brought into being by the word of a god, who when he uttered any name caused the object thereby to exist. Thoth is the principal creator by this means and this idea probably belongs to a period soon after the age of the animal gods.

(2) The other view is that Ptah framed the world as an artificer, with the aid of eight Khnumu, or earth-gnomes. This belongs to the theology of the abstract gods. The primitive people seem to have been content with the eternity of matter, and only personified nature when they described space, Shu, as separating the sky, Nut, from the earth, Seb. This is akin to the separation of chaos into sky and sea in Genesis.

The sun is called the egg laid by the primeval goose; and in later time this was said to be laid by a god, or modelled by Ptah. Evidently this goose egg is a primitive tale which was adapted to later theology.

The sky is said to be upheld by four pillars. These were later connected. with the gods of the four quarters; but the primitive four pillars were represented together, with the capitals one over the other, in the sign dad, the emblem of stability. These may have belonged to the Osiris cycle, as he is "lord of the pillars," daddu, and his center in the Delta was named Daddu from the pillars. The setting up of the pillars or dad emblem was a great festival in which the kings took part, and which is often represented.

The creation of life was variously attributed to different great gods where they were worshipped. Khnumu, Osiris, Amen, or Atmu, each are stated to be the creator. The mode was only defined by the theorists of Heliopolis; they imagined that Atmu self-produced Seb and Nut, and they in turn other gods, from whom at last sprang mankind. But this is merely later theorizing to fit a theology in being.

The cosmogonic theories, therefore, were by no means important articles of belief, but rather assumptions of what the gods were likely to have done similar to the acts of men. The creation by the word is the more elevated idea, and is parallel to the creation in Genesis.

The conception of the nature of the world was that of a great plain, over which the sun passed by day, and beneath which it travelled through the hours of night. The movement of the sun was supposed to be that of floating on the heavenly ocean, figured by its being in a boat, which was probably an expression for its flotation. The elaboration of the nature of the regions through which the sun passed at night essentially belongs to the Ra theology, and only recognises the kingdom of Osiris by placing it in one of the hours of night. The old conception of the dim realm of the cemetery-god Seker occupies the fourth and fifth hours; the sixth hour is an approach to the Osiride region, and the seventh hour is the kingdom of Osiris. Each hour was separated by gates, which were guarded by demons who needed to be controlled by magic formulæ.

THE GODS OF ANCIENT EGYPT

Before dealing with the special varieties of the Egyptians' belief in gods, it is best to try to avoid a misunderstanding of their whole conception of the supernatural. The term god has come to tacitly imply to our minds such a highly specialized group of attributes that we can hardly throw our ideas back into the more remote conceptions to which we also attach the same name. It is unfortunate that every other word for supernatural intelligences has become debased, so that we cannot well speak of demons, devils, ghosts, or fairies without implying a noxious or a trifling meaning, quite unsuited to the ancient deities that were so beneficent and powerful. If then we use the word god for such conceptions, it must always be with the reservation that the word has now a very different meaning from what it had to ancient minds.

To the Egyptian the gods might be mortal; even Ra, the sun-god, is said to have grown old and feeble, Osiris was slain, and Orion, the great hunter of the heavens, killed and ate the gods. The mortality of gods has been dwelt on by Dr. Frazer in the "Golden Bough," and the many instances of tombs of gods, and of the slaying of the deified man who was worshipped, all show that immortality was not a divine attribute. Nor was there any doubt that they might suffer while alive; one myth tells how Ra, as he walked on earth, was bitten by a magic serpent and suffered torments. The gods were also supposed to share in a life like that of man, not only in Egypt but in most ancient lands. Offerings of food and drink were constantly supplied to them, in Egypt laid upon the altars, in other lands burnt for a sweet savour. At Thebes the divine wife of the god, or high priestess, was the head of the harem of concubines of the god; and similarly in Babylonia the chamber of the god with the golden couch could only be visited by the priestess who slept there for oracular responses. The Egyptian gods could not be cognisant of what passed on earth without being informed, nor could they reveal their will at a distant place except by sending a messenger; they were as limited as the Greek gods who required the aid of Iris to communicate one with another or with mankind. The gods, therefore, have no divine superiority to man in conditions or limitations; they can only be described as pre-existent, acting intelligences, with scarcely greater powers than man might hope to gain by magic or witchcraft of his own. This conception explains how easily the divine merged into the human in Greek theology, and how frequently divine ancestors occurred in family histories. (By the word "theology" is designated the knowledge about gods.)

There are in ancient theologies very different classes of gods. Some races, as the modern Hindu, revel in a profusion of gods and godlings, which are continually being increased. Others, as the Turanians, whether Sumerian Babylonians, modern Siberians, or Chinese, do not adopt the worship of great gods, but deal with a host of animistic spirits, ghosts, devils, or whatever we may call them; and Shamanism or witchcraft is their system for conciliating such adversaries. But all our knowledge of the early positions and nature of great gods shows them to have stood on an entirely different footing to these varied spirits. Were the conception of a god only an evolution from such spirit worship of one god, polytheism would precede monotheism in each tribe or race. What we actually find is the contrary of this, monotheism is the first stage traceable in theology. Hence we must rather look on the theologic conception of the Aryan and Semitic races as quite apart from the demon-worship of the Turanians. Indeed the Chinese seem to have a mental aversion to the conception of a personal god, and to think either of the host of earth spirits and other demons, or else of the pantheistic abstraction of heaven.

Wherever we can trace back polytheism to its earliest stages we find that it results from combinations of monotheism. In Egypt even Osiris, Isis, and Horus - so familiar as a triad - are found at first as separate units in different places, Isis as a virgin goddess, and Horus as a self-existent god. Each city appears to have but one god belonging to it, to whom others were added. Similarly in Babylonia each great city had its supreme god; and the combinations of these, and their transformations in order to form them in groups when their homes were politically united, show how essentially they were solitary deities at first.

Not only must we widely distinguish the demonology of races worshipping numerous earth spirits and demons from the theology of races devoted to solitary great gods; but we must further distinguish the varying ideas of the latter class. Most of the theologic races have no objection to tolerating the worship of other gods side by side with that of their own local deity. It is in this way that the compound theologies built up the polytheism of Egypt and of Greece. But others of the theologic races have the conception of "a jealous god," who would not tolerate the presence of a rival. We cannot date this conception earlier than Mosaism, and this idea struggled hard against polytheistic toleration. This view acknowledges the reality of other gods, but ignores their claims. The still later view was that other gods were non-existent, a position started by the Hebrew prophets in contempt of idolatry, scarcely grasped by early Christianity, but triumphantly held by Islam.

We therefore have to deal with the following conceptions, which fall into two main groups, that probably belong to different divisions of mankind:

Animism
Demonology

Tribal Monotheism	*At any state the unity of different gods may be accepted as a modus vivendi or as a philosophy.*
Combinations (forming tolerant Polytheism)	*Ditto*
Jealous Monotheism	*Ditto*
Sole Monotheism	*Ditto*

All of these require mention here as more or less of each principle, both of animism and monotheism, can be traced in the innumerable combinations found during the six thousand years of Egyptian religion: these combinations of beliefs being due to combinations of the races to which they belonged.

Before we can understand what were the relations between man and the gods we must first notice the conceptions of the nature of man. In the prehistoric days of Egypt the position and direction of the body was always the same in every burial; offerings of food and drink were placed by it, figures of servants, furniture, even games, were included in the grave. It must be concluded therefore that it was a belief in immortality which gave rise to such a detailed ritual of the dead, though we have no written evidence upon this.

So soon as we reach the age of documents we find on tombstones that the person is denoted by the khu between the arms of the ka. From later writings it is seen that the khu is applied to a spirit of man; while the ka is not the body but the activities of sense and perception. Thus, in the earliest age of documents, two entities were believed to vitalize the body.

The KA is more frequently named than any other part, as all funeral offerings were made for the KA. It is said that if opportunities of satisfaction in life were missed it is grievous to the ka, and that the ka must not be annoyed needlessly; hence it was more than perception, and it included all that we might call consciousness. Perhaps we may grasp it best as the "self," with the same variety of meaning that we have in our own word. The ka was represented as a human being following after the man; it was born at the same time as the man, but persisted after death and lived in and about the tomb. It could act and visit other kas after death, but it could not resist the least touch of physical force. It was always represented by two upraised arms, the acting parts of the person. Beside the ka of man, all objects likewise had their kas, which were comparable to the human ka, and among these the ka lived. This view leads closely to the world of ideas permeating the material world in later philosophy.

The KHU is figured as a crested bird, which has the meaning of "glorious" or "shining" in ordinary use. It refers to a less material conception than the ka, and may be called the intelligence or spirit.

The KHAT is the material body of man which was the vehicle of the KA, and inhabited by the KHU.

The BA belongs to, a different pneumatology to that just noticed. It is the soul apart from the body, figured as a human-headed bird. The conception probably arose from the white owls, with round beads and every human expressions, which frequent the tombs, flying noiselessly to and fro. The ba required food and drink, which were provided for it by the goddess of the cemetery. It thus overlaps the scope of the ka, and probably belongs to a different race to that which define the man.

The sahu or mummy is associated particularly with the ba; and the ba bird is often shown as resting on the mummy or seeking to re-enter it.

The khaybet was the shadow of a man; the importance of the shadow in early ideas is well known.

The sekhem was the force or ruling power of man, but is rarely mentioned.

The ab is the will and intentions, symbolised by the heart; often used in phrases such as a man being "in the heart of his lord," "wideness of heart" for satisfaction, "washing of the heart" for giving vent to temper.

The HATI is the physical heart, the "chief" organ of the body, also wed metaphorically.

The ran is the name which was essential to man, as also to inanimate things. Without a name nothing really existed. The knowledge. of the name gave power over its owner; a great myth turns on Isis obtaining the name of Ra by stratagem, and thus getting the two eyes of Ra - the sun and moon - for her son Horus. Both in ancient and modern races the knowledge of the real name of a man is carefully guarded, and often secondary names are used for secular purposes. It was usual for Egyptians to have a "great name" and a "little name"; the great name is often compounded with that of a god or a king, and was very probably reserved for religious purposes, as it is only found on religious and funerary monuments.

We must not suppose by any means that all of these parts of the person were equally important, or were believed in simultaneously. The ka, khu, and khat seem to form one group; the ba and sehu belong to another; the ab, hati, and sekhem are hardly more than metaphors, such as we commonly use; the khaybet is a later idea which probably belongs to the system of animism and witchcraft, where the shadow gave a hold upon the man. The ran, name, belongs partly to the same system, but also is the germ of the later philosophy of idea.

The purpose of religion to the Egyptian was to secure the favor of the god. There is but little trace of negative prayer to avert evils or deprecate evil influences, but rather of positive prayer for concrete favors. On the part of kings this is usually of the Jacob type, offering to provide temples and services to the god in return for material prosperity. The Egyptian was essentially self-satisfied, he had no confession to make of sin or wrong, and had no thought of pardon. In the judgment he boldly averred that he was free of the forty-two sins that might prevent his entry into the kingdom of Osiris. If he failed to establish his innocence in the weighing of his heart, there was no other plea, but he was consumed by fire and by a hippopotamus, and no hope remained for him.

The various beliefs of the Egyptians regarding the future life are so distinct from each other and so incompatible, that they may be classified into groups more readily than the theology; thus they serve to indicate the varied sources of the religion.

The most simple form of belief was that of the continued existence of the soul in the tomb and about the cemetery. In upper Egypt at present a hole is left at the top of the tomb chamber; and I have seen a woman remove the covering of the hole, and talk down to her deceased husband. Also funeral offerings of food and drink, and even beds, are still placed in the tombs. A similar feeling, without any precise beliefs, doubtless prompted the earlier forms of provision for the dead. The soul wandered around the tomb seeking sustenance, and was fed by the goddess who dwelt in the thick sycamore trees that overshadowed the cemetery. She is represented as pouring out drink for the ba and holding a tray of cakes for it to feed upon. In the grave we find this belief shown by the jars of water, wine, and perhaps other liquids, the stores of corn, the geese, haunches and heads of oxen, the cakes, and dates, and pomegranates which were laid by the dead. In an early king's tomb there might be many rooms full of these offerings. There were also the weapons for defence and for the chase, the toilet objects, the stores of clothing, the draughtsmen, and even the literature of papyri buried with the dead. The later form of this system was the representation of all these offerings in sculpture and drawing in the tomb. This modification probably belongs to the belief in the ka, which could be supported by the ka of the food and use the ka of the various objects, the figures of the objects being supposed to provide the kas of them. This system is entirely complete in itself, and does not presuppose or require any theologic connection. It might well belong to an age of simple animism, and be a survival of that in later times.

The greatest theologic system was that of the kingdom of Osiris. This was a counterpart of the earthly life, but was reserved for the worthy. All the dead belonged to Osiris and were brought before him for judgment. The protest of being innocent of the forty-two sins was made, and then the heart was weighed against truth, symbolised by the ostrich feather, the emblem of the goddess of truth. From this feather, the emblem of lightness, being placed against the heart in weighing, it seems that sins were considered to weigh down the heart, and its lightness required to be proved. Thoth, the god who recorded the weighing, then stated that the soul left the judgment hall true of voice with his heart and members restored to him, and that he should follow Osiris in his kingdom. This kingdom of Osiris was at first thought of as being in the marsh lands of the Delta; when these became familiar it was transferred to Syria, and finally to the northeast of the sky, where the milky way became the heavenly Nile. The main occupation in this kingdom was agriculture, as on earth; the souls ploughed the land, sowed the corn, and reaped the harvest of heavenly maize, taller and fatter than any of this world. In this land they rowed on the heavenly streams, they sat in shady arbors, and played the games which they had loved. But the cultivation was a toil, and therefore it was to be done by numerous serfs. In the beginning of the monarchy it seems that the servants of the king were all buried around him to serve him in the future; from the second to the twelfth dynasty we lose sight of this idea, and then we find slave figures buried in the tombs. These figures were provided with the hoe for tilling the soil, the pick for breaking the clods, a basket for carrying the earth, a pot for watering the crops, and they were inscribed with an order to respond for their master when he was called on to work in the fields. In the eighteenth dynasty the figures sometimes have actual tool models buried with them; but usually the tools are in relief or painted on the figure. This idea continued until the less material view of the future life arose in Greek times; then the deceased man was said to have "gone to Osiris" in such a year of his age, but no slave figures were laid with him. This view of the future is complete in itself, and is appropriately provided for in the tomb.

A third view of the future life belongs to an entirely different theologic system, that of the progress of the sun-god Ra. According to this the soul went to join the setting sun in the west, and prayed to be allowed to enter the boat of the sun in the company of the gods; thus it would be taken along in everlasting light, and saved from the terrors and demons of the night over which the sun triumphed. No occupations were predicated of this future; simply to rest in the divine company was the entire purpose, and the successful repelling of the powers of darkness in each hour of the night by means of spells was the only activity. To provide for the solar journey a model boat was placed in the tomb with the figures of boatmen, to enable the dead to sail with the sun, or to reach the solar bark. This view of the future implied a journey to the west, and hence came the belief in the soul setting out to cross the desert westward. We find also an early god of the dead, Khent-amenti, "he who is in the west," probably arising from this same view. This god was later identified with Osiris when the fusion of the two theories of the soul arose. At Abydos Khent-amenti only is named at first, and Osiris does not appear until later times, though that cemetery came to be regarded as specially dedicated to Osiris.

Now in all these views that we have named there is no occasion for preserving the body. It is the Ba that is fed in the cemetery not the body. It is an immaterial body that takes part in the kingdom of Osiris, in the sky. It is an immaterial body that can accompany the gods in the boat of the sun. There is so far no call to conserve the body by the peculiar mummification which first appears in the early dynasties. The dismemberment of the bones, and removal of the flesh, which was customary in the prehistoric times, and survived down to the fifth dynasty, would accord with any of these theories, all of which were probably pre-dynastic. But the careful mummifying of the body became customary only in the third or fourth dynasty, and is therefore later than the theories that we have noticed. The idea of thus preserving the body seems to look forward to some later revival of it on earth, rather than to a personal life immediately after death. The funeral accompaniment of this view was the abundance of amulets placed on various parts of the body to preserve it. A few amulets are found worn on a necklace or bracelet in early times; but the full development of the amulet system was in the twenty-sixth to thirtieth dynasties.

We have tried to disentangle the diverse types of belief, by seeing what is incompatible between them. But in practice we find every form of mixture of these views in most ages. In the prehistoric times the preservation of the bones, but not of the flesh, was constant; and food offerings show that at least the theory of the soul wandering in the cemetery was familiar. Probably the Osiris theory is also of the later prehistoric times, as the myth of Osiris is certainly older than the dynasties. The Ra worship was associated specially with Heliopolis, and may have given rise to the union with Ra also before the dynasties, when Heliopolis was probably a capital of the kings of lower Egypt. The boats figured on the prehistoric tomb at Hierakonpolis bear this out. In the first dynasty there is no mummy known, funeral offerings abound, and the khu and ka are named. Our documents do not give any evidence, then, of the Osiris and Ra theories. In the pyramid period the king was called the Osiris, and this view is the leading one in the pyramid inscriptions, yet the Ra theory is also incompatibly present; the body is mummified; but funeral offerings of food seem to have much diminished. In the eighteenth and nineteenth dynasties the Ra theory gained ground greatly over the Osirian; and the basis of all the views of the future is almost entirely the union with Ra during the night and day. The mummy and amulet theory was not dominant; but the funeral offerings somewhat increased. The twenty-sixth dynasty almost dropped the Ra theory; the Osirian kingdom and its population of slave figures is the most familiar view, and the preservation of the body by amulets was essential. Offerings of food rarely appear in these later times. This dominance of Osiris leads on to the anthropomorphic worship, which interacts on the growth of Christianity as we shall see further. Lastly, when all the theologic views of the future had perished, the oldest idea of all, food, drink, and rest for the dead, has still kept its hold upon the feelings of the people in spite of the teachings of Islam.

THE WORSHIP OF ANIMALS IN ANCIENT EGYPT

The worship of animals has been known in many countries; but in Egypt it was maintained to a later pitch of civilization than elsewhere, and the mixture of such a primitive system with more elevated beliefs seemed as strange to the Greek as it does to us. The original motive was a kinship of animals with man, much like that underlying the system of totems. Each place or tribe had its sacred species that was linked with the tribe; the life of the species was carefully preserved, excepting in the one example selected for worship, which after a given time was killed and sacramentally eaten by the tribe. This was certainly the case with the bull at Memphis and the ram at Thebes. That it was the whole species that was sacred, at one place or another, is shown by the penalties for killing any animal of the species, by the wholesale burial and even mummifying of every example, and by the plural form of the names of the gods later connected with the animals, Heru, hawks, Khnumu, rams, etc.

In the prehistoric times the serpent was sacred; figures of the coiled serpent were hung up in the house and worn as an amulet; similarly in historic times a figure of the agathodemon serpent was placed in a temple of Amen-hotep III at Benha. In the first dynasty the serpent was figured in pottery, as a fender around the hearth. The hawk also appears in many pre-dynastic figures, large and small, both worn on the person and carried as standards. The lion is found both in life-size temple figures, lesser objects of worship, and personal amulets. The scorpion was similarly honored in the prehistoric ages.

It is difficult to separate now between animals which were worshipped quite independently, and those which were associated as emblems of anthropomorphic gods. Probably we shall be right in regarding both classes of animals as having been sacred at a remote time, and the connection with the human form as being subsequent. The ideas connected with the animals were those of their most prominent characteristics; hence it appears that it was for the sake of the character that each animal was worshipped, and not because of any fortuitous association with a tribe.

The baboon was regarded as the emblem of Tahuti, the god of wisdom; the serious expression and human ways of the large baboons are an obvious cause for their being regarded as the wisest of animals. Tahuti is represented as a baboon from the first dynasty down to late times, and four baboons were sacred in his temple at Hemmopolis. These four baboons were often portrayed as adoring the sun; this idea is due to their habit of chattering at sunrise.

The lioness appears in the compound figures of the goddesses Sekhet, Bast, Mahes, and Tefnut. In the form of Sekhet the lioness is the destructive power of Ra, the sun: it is Sekhet who, in the legend, destroys mankind from Herakleopolis to Heliopolis at the bidding of Ra. The other lioness goddesses are probably likewise destructive or hunting deities. The lesser felidæ also appear; the cheetah and serval are sacred to Hathor in Sinai; the small cats are sacred to Bast, especially at Speos Artemidos and Bubastis.

The bull was sacred in many places, and his worship underlay that of the human gods, who were said to be incarnated in him. The idea is that of the fighting power, as when the king is figured as a bull trampling on his enemies, and the reproductive power, as in the title of the self-renewing gods, "bull of his mother." The most renowned was the Hapi or Apis bull of Memphis, in whom Ptah was said to be incarnate and who was Osirified and became the Osir-hapi.

Thus appears to have originated the great Ptolemaic god Serapis, as certainly the mausoleum of the bulls was the Serapeum of the Greeks. Another bull of a more massive breed was the Ur-mer or Mnevis of Heliopolis, in whom Ra was incarnate. A third bull was Bakh or Bakis of Hermonthis the incarnation of Mentu. And a fourth bull, Kan-nub or Kanobos, was worshipped at the city of that name. The cow was identified with Hathor, who appears with cow's ears and horns, and who is probably the cow-goddess Ashtaroth or Istar of Asia. Isis, as identified with Hathor, is also joined in this connection.

The ram was also worshipped as a procreative god; at Mendes in the Delta identified with Osiris, at Herakleopolis identified with Hershefi, at Thebes as Amon, and at the Cataract as Khnumu the creator. The association of the ram with Amon was strongly held by the Ethiopians; and in the Greek tale of Nektanebo, the last Pharaoh, having by magic visited Olympias and become the father of Alexander, he came as the incarnation of Amon wearing the ram's skin.

The hippopotamus was the goddess Ta-urt, "the great one," the patroness of pregnancy, who is never shown in any other form. Rarely this animal appears as the emblem of the god Set.

The jackal haunted the cemeteries on the edge of the desert, and so came to be taken as the guardian of the dead, and identified with Anubis, the god of departing souls. Another aspect of the jackal was as the maker of tracks in the desert; the jackal paths are the best guides to practicable courses, avoiding the valleys and precipices, and so the animal was known as Up-uat, "the opener of ways," who showed the way for the dead across the western desert. Species of dogs seem to have been held sacred and mummified on merely the general ground of confusion with the jackal. The ichneumon and the shrewmouse were also held sacred, though not identified with a human god.

The hawk was the principal sacred bird, and was identified with Horus and Ra, the sun-god. It was mainly worshipped at Edfu and Hierakonpolis. The souls of kings were supposed to fly up to heaven in the form of hawks, perhaps due to the kingship originating in the hawk district in upper Egypt. Seker, the god of the dead, appears as a mummified hawk, and on his boat are many small hawks, perhaps the souls of kings who have joined him. The mummy hawk is also Sopdu, the god of the east.

The vulture was the emblem of maternity, as being supposed to care especially for her young. Hence she is identified with Mut, the mother goddess of Thebes. The queen-mothers have vulture head-dresses; the vulture is shown hovering over kings to protect them, and a row of spread-out vultures are figured on the roofs of the tomb passages to protect the soul. The ibis was identified with Tahuti, the god of Hermopolis. The goose is connected with Amon of Thebes. The swallow was also sacred.

The crocodile was worshipped especially in the Fayum, where it frequented the marshy levels of the great lake, and Strabo's description of the feeding of the sacred crocodile there is familiar. It was also worshipped at Onuphis; and at Nubti or Ombos it was identified with Set, and held sacred. Beside the name of Sebek or Soukhos in Fayum, it was there identified with Osiris as the western god of the dead. The frog was an emblem of the goddess Heqt, but was not worshipped.

The cobra serpent was sacred from the earliest times to the present day. It was never identified with any of the great deities, but three goddesses appear in serpent form: Uazet, the Delta goddess of Buto; Mert-seger, "the lover of silence," the goddess of the Theban necropolis; and Rannut, the harvest goddess. The memory of great pythons of the prehistoric days appears in the serpent-necked monsters on the slate palettes at the beginning of the monarchy, and the immense serpent Agap of the underworld in the later mythology. The serpent has however been a popular object of worship apart from specific gods. We have already noted it on prehistoric amulets, and coiled round the hearths of the early dynasties. Serpents were mummified; and when we reach the full evidences of popular worship, in the terra-cotta figures and jewellery of later times, the serpent is very prominent. There were usually two represented together, one often with the head of Serapis, the other of Isis, so therefore male and female. Down to modern times a serpent is worshipped at Sheykh Heridy, and miraculous cures attributed to it (S. R. E. B. 213).

Various fishes were sacred, as the Oxyrhynkhos, Phagros, Lepidotos, Latos, and others; but they were not identified with gods, and we do not know of their being worshipped. The scorpion was the emblem of the goddess Selk, and is found in prehistoric amulets; but it is not known to have been adored, and most usually it represents evils, where Horus is shown overcoming noxious creatures.

It will be observed that nearly all of the animals which were worshipped had qualities for which they were noted, and in connection with which they were venerated. If the animal worship were due to totemism, or a sense of animal brotherhood in certain tribes, we must also assume that that was due to these qualities of the animal; whereas totemism in other countries does not seem to be due to veneration of special qualities of the animals. It is therefore more likely that the animal worship simply arose from the nature of the animals, and not from any true totemism, although each animal came to be associated with the worship of a particular tribe or district.

THE GROUPS OF GODS

In a country which has been subjected to so many inflows of various peoples as has Egypt, it is to be expected that there would be a great diversity of deities and a complex and inconsistent theology. To discriminate the principal classes of conceptions of gods is the first step toward understanding the growth of the systems. The broad diversion of animal gods and human gods is obvious; and the mixed type of human figures with animal heads is clearly an adaptation of the animal gods to the later conception of a human god. Another valuable separator lies in the compound. names of gods. It is impossible to suppose a people uniting two gods, both of which belonged to them aboriginally; there would be no reason for two similar gods in a single system, and we never hear in classical mythology of Hermes-Apollo or Pallas-Artemis, while Zeus is compounded with half of the barbarian gods of Asia. So in Egypt, when we find such compounds as Amon-Ra, or Ptah-Sokar-Osiris, we have the certainty that each name in the compound is derived from a different race, and that a unifying operation has taken place on gods that belonged to entirely different sources.

We must beware of reading our modern ideas into the ancient views. As we noticed in an earlier part of this chapter, each tribe or locality seems to have had but one god originally; certainly the more remote our view, the more separate are the gods. Hence to the people of any one district "the god" was a distinctive name for their own god; and it would have seemed as strange to discriminate him from the surrounding gods, as it would to a Christian in Europe if he specified that he did not mean Allah or Siva or Heaven when he speaks of God. Hence we find generic descriptions used in place of the god's name, as "lord of heaven," or "mistress of turquoise," while it is certain that specific gods as Osiris or Hathor are in view. A generic name "god" or "the god" no more implies that the Egyptians recognised a unity of all the gods, than "god" in the Old Testament implies that Yahvah was one with Chemosh and Baal. The simplicity of the term only shows that no other object of adoration was in view.

We have already noticed the purely animal gods; following on these we now shall describe those which were combined with a human form, then those which are purely human in their character, next those which are nature gods, and lastly those which are an abstract character.

Animal-headed Gods: Beside the worship of species of animals, which we have noticed in the last chapter, certain animals were combined with the human form. It was always the head of the animal which was united to a human body; the only converse instance of a human head on an animal body - the sphinxes - represented the king and not a god. Possibly the combination arose from priests wearing the heads of animals when personating the god, as the high priest wore the ram's skin when personating Amon. But when we notice the frequent combinations and love of symbolism, shown upon the early carvings, the union of the ancient sacred animal with the human form is quite in keeping with the views and feelings of the primitive Egyptians. Many of these composite gods never emerged from the animal connection, and these we must regard as belonging to the earlier stage of theology.

Seker was a Memphite god of the dead, independent of the worship of Osiris and of Ptah, for he was combined with them as Ptah-Seker-Osiris; as he maintained a place there in the face of the great worship of Ptah, he was probably an older god, and this is indicated by his having an entirely animal form down to a late date. The sacred bark of Seker bore his figure as that of a mummified hawk; and along the boat is a row of hawks which probably are the spirits of deceased kings who have joined Seker in his journey to the world of the dead. As there are often two allied forms of the same root, one written with k and the other with g," [3] it seems probable that Seker, the funeral god of Memphis, is allied to

Mert Seger (lover of silence). She was the funeral god of Thebes, and was usually figured as a serpent. From being only known in animal form, and unconnected with any of the elaborated theology, it seems that we have in this goddess a primitive deity of the dead. It appears, then, that the gods of the great cemeteries were known as Silence and the Lover of Silence, and both come down from the age of animal deities. Seker became in late times changed into a hawk-headed human figure.

Two important deities of early times were Nekhebt, the vulture goddess of the southern kingdom, centred at Hierakonpolis, and Uazet, the serpent goddess of the northern kingdom, centred at Buto. These appear in all ages as the emblems of the two kingdoms, frequently as supporters on either side of the royal names; in later times they appear as human goddesses crowning the king.

Khnumu, the creator, was the great god of the cataract. He is shown as making man upon the potter's wheel; and in a tale he is said to frame a woman. He must belong to a different source from that of Ptah or Ra, and was the creative principle in the period of animal gods, as he is almost always shown with the head of a ram. He was popular down to late times, where amulets of his figure are often found.

Tahuti, or Thôth, was the god of writing and learning, and was the chief deity of Hermopolis. He almost always has the head of an ibis, the bird sacred to him. The baboon is also a frequent emblem of his, but he is never figured with the baboon head. The ibis appears standing upon a shrine as early as on a tablet of Mena; Thôth is the constant recorder in scenes of the judgment, and he appears down to Roman times as the patron of scribes. The eighteenth dynasty of kings incorporated his name as Thôthmes, "born of Thôth," owing to their Hermopolite origin.

Skhmet is the lion goddess, who represents the fierceness of the sun's heat. She appears in the myth of the destruction of mankind as slaughtering the enemies of Ra. Her only form is that with the head of a lioness. But she blends imperceptibly with

Bastet, who has the head of a cat. She was the goddess of Pa-bast or Bubastis, and in her honor immense festivals were there held. Her name is found in the beginning of the pyramid times; but her main period of popularity was that of the Shisaks who ruled from Bubastis, and in the later times images of her were very frequent as amulets. It is possible from the name that this feline goddess, whose foreign origin is acknowledged, was the female form of the god Bes, who is dressed in a lion's skin, and also came in from the east.

Mentu was the hawk-god of Erment south of Thebes, who became in the eighteenth to twentieth dynasties especially the god of war. He appears with the hawk head, or sometimes as a hawk-headed sphinx; and he became confused with Ra and with Amon.

Sebek is figured as a man with the crocodile's head; but he has no theologic importance, and always remained the local god of certain districts.

Heqt, the goddess symbolised by the frog, was the patron of birth, and assisted in the infancy of the kings. She was a popular and general deity not mainly associated with particular places.

Hershefi was the ram-headed god of Herakleopolis, but is never found outside of that region.

We now come to three animal-headed gods who became associated with the great Osiride group of human gods. Set or Setesh was the god of the prehistoric inhabitants before the coming in of Horus. He is always shown with the head of a fabulous animal, having upright square ears and a long nose. When in entirely animal form he has a long upright tail. The dog-like animal is the earliest type, as in the second dynasty; but later the human form with animal head prevailed. His worship underwent great fluctuations. At first he was the great god of all Egypt; but his worshippers were gradually driven out by the followers of Horus, as described in a semi-mythical history. Then he appears strongly in the second dynasty, the last king of which united the worship of Set and Horus. After suppression he appears in favor in the early eighteenth dynasty; and even gave the name to Sety I and II of the nineteenth dynasty. His part in the Osiris myth will be noted below.

Anpu or Anubis was originally the jackal guardian of the cemetery, and the leader of the dead in the other world. Nearly all the early funeral formulæ mention Anpu on his hill, or Anpu lord of the underworld. As the patron of the dead he naturally took a place in the myth of Osiris, the god of the dead, and appears as leading the soul into the judgment of Osiris.

Horus was the hawk-god of upper Egypt, especially of Edfu and Hierakonpolis. Though originally an independent god, and even keeping apart as Hor-ur, "Horus the elder," throughout later times, yet he was early mingled with the Osiris myth, probably as the ejector of Set who was also the enemy of Osiris. He is sometimes entirely in hawk form; more usually with a hawk's head, and in later times he appears as the infant son of Isis entirely human in form. His special function is that of overcoming evil; in the earliest days the conqueror of Set, later as the subduer of noxious animals, figured on a very popular amulet, and lastly, in Roman times, as a hawk-headed warrior on horseback slaying a dragon, thus passing into the type of St. George. He also became mingled with early Christian ideas; and the lock of hair of Horus attached to the cross originated the chi rho monogram of Christ.

We have now passed briefly over the principal gods which combined the animal and human forms. We see how the animal form is generally the older, and how it was apparently independent of the human form, which has been attached to it by a more anthropomorphic people. We see that all of these gods must be accredited to the second stratum, if not, to the earliest formation, of religion in Egypt. And we must associate with this theology the cemetery theory of the soul which preceded that of the Osiris or Ra religions.

We now turn to the deities which are always represented in human form, and never associated with animal figures; neither do they originate in a cosmic - or nature - worship, nor in abstract idea. There are three divisions of this class, the Osiris family, the Amon family, and the goddess Neit.

GODS IN HUMAN FORM

Osiris - Asar or Asir - is the most familiar figure of the pantheon, but it is mainly on late sources that we have to depend for the myth; and his worship was so much adapted to harmonize with other ideas, that care is needed to trace his true position. The Osiride portions of the Book of the Dead are certainly very early, and precede the solar portions, though both views were already mingled in the pyramid texts. We cannot doubt but that the Osiris worship reaches back to the prehistoric age. In the earliest tombs offering to Anubis is named, for whom Osiris became substituted in the fifth and sixth dynasties. In the pyramid times we only find that kings are termed Osiris, having undergone their apotheoisis at the sed festival; but in the eighteenth dynasty and onward every justified person was entitled the Osiris, as being united with the god. His worship was unknown at Abydos in the earlier temples, and is not mentioned at the cataracts; though in later times he became the leading deity of Abydos and of Philæ. Thus in all directions the recognition of Osiris continued to increase; but, looking at the antiquity of his cult, we must recognize in this change the gradual triumph of a popular religion over a state religion which had been superimposed upon it. The earliest phase of Osirism that we can identify is in portions of the Book of the Dead. These assume the kingdom of Osiris, and a judgment preceding admission to the blessed future; the completely human character of Osiris and his family are implied, and there is no trace of animal or nature worship belonging to him. How far the myth, as recorded in Roman times by Plutarch, can be traced to earlier and later sources is very uncertain. The main outlines, which may be primitive, are as follows. Osiris was a civilising king of Egypt, who was murdered by his brother Set and seventy-two conspirators. Isis, his wife, found the coffin of Osiris at Byblos in Syria and brought it to Egypt. Set then tore up the body of Osiris and scattered it. Isis sought the fragments, and built a shrine over each of them. Isis and Horus then attacked Set and drove him from Egypt, and finally down the Red Sea. In other aspects Osiris seems to have been a corn god, and the scattering of his body in Egypt is like the well-known division of the sacrifice to the corn god, and the burial of parts in separate fields to ensure their fertility.

How we are to analyse the formation of the early myths is suggested by the known changes of later times. When two tribes who worshipped different (rods fought together and one overcame the other, the god of the conqueror is always considered to have overcome the god of the vanquished. The struggle of Horus and Set is expressly stated on the Temple of Edfu to have been a tribal war, in which the followers of Horus overcame those of Set, established garrisons and forges at various places down the Nile Valley, and finally ousted the Set party from the whole land. We can hardly therefore avoid reading the history of the animosities of the gods as being the struggles of their worshippers.

If we try to trace the historic basis of the Osiris myth, we must take into account the early customs and ideas among which the myths arose. The cutting up of the body was the regular ritual of the prehistoric people, and, even as late as the fifth dynasty, the bones were separately treated, and even wrapped up separately when the body was reunited for burial. We must also notice the apotheosis festival of the king, which was probably his sacrificial death and union with the god, in the prehistoric age. The course of events which might have served as the basis for the Osiris myth may then have been somewhat as follows. Osiris was the god of a tribe which occupied a large part of Egypt. The kings of this tribe were sacrificed after thirty years' reign - like the killing of kings at fixed intervals elsewhere - and they thus became the Osiris himself. Their bodies were dismembered, as usual at that period, the flesh ceremonially eaten by the assembled people - as was done in prehistoric times - and the bones distributed among the various centres of the tribe, the head to Abydos, the neck, spine, limbs, etc., to various places of which there were fourteen in all. The worshippers of Set broke in upon this people, stopped this worship, or killed Osiris, as was said, and established the dominion of their animal god. They were in turn attacked by the Isis worshippers, who joined the older population of the Osiris tribe, reopened the shrines, and established Osiris worship again. The Set tribe returning in force attacked the Osiris tribe and scattered all the relies of the shrines in every part of the land. To re-establish their power, the Osiris and Isis tribes called in the worshippers of the hawk Horus, who were old enemies of the Set tribe, and with their help finally expelled the Set worshippers from the whole country. Such a history, somewhat misunderstood in a later age when the sacrifice of kings and anthropophagy was forgotten, would give the basis for nearly all the features of the Osiris myth as recorded in Roman times.

If we try to materialize this history more closely, we see that the Osiris worshippers occupied both the Delta and upper Egypt, and that fourteen important centres were recognised at the earliest time, which afterwards became the capitals of nomes, and were added to until they numbered forty-two divisions in later ages. Set was the god of the Asiatic invaders who broke in upon this civilization; and about a quarter through the long ages of the prehistoric culture, perhaps 7500 B.C., we find material evidences of considerable changes brought in from the

Arabian or Semitic side. It may not be unlikely that this was the first triumph of Set. The Isis worshippers came from the Delta, where Isis was worshipped at Buto as a virgin goddess, apart from Osiris or Horus. These followers of Isis succeeded in helping the rest of the early Libyan inhabitants to resist the Set worship, and re-establish Osiris. The close of the prehistoric age is marked by a great decline in work and abilities, very likely due to more trouble from Asia, when Set scattered the relies of Osiris. Lastly we cannot avoid seeing in the Horus triumph the conquest of Egypt by the dynastic race who came down from the district of Edfu and Hierakonpolis, the centres of Horus worship; and helped the older inhabitants to drive out the Asiatics. Nearly the same chain of events is seen in later times, when the Berber king Aahmes I helped the Egyptians to expel the Hyksos. If we can thus succeed in connecting the archæology of the prehistoric age with the history preserved in the myths, it shows that Osiris must have been the national god as early as the beginning of prehistoric culture. His civilizing mission may well have been the introduction of cultivation, at about 8000 B.C., into the Nile Valley.

The theology of Osiris was at first that of a god of those holy fields in which the souls of the dead enjoyed a future fife. There was necessarily some selection to exclude the wicked from such happiness, and Osiris judged each soul whether it were worthy. This judgment became elaborated in detailed scenes, where Isis and Neb-hat stand behind Osiris who is on his throne, Anubis leads in the soul, the heart is placed in the balance, and Thôth stands to weigh it and to record the result. The occupation of the souls in this future we have noticed in an earlier part of this chapter. The function of Osiris was therefore the reception and rule of the dead, and we never find him as a god of action or patronizing any of the affairs of life.

Isis - Aset or Isit - became attached at a very early time to the Osiris worship; and appears in later myths as the sister and wife of Osiris. But she always remained on a very different plane to Osiris. Her worship and priesthood were far more popular than those of Osiris, and she appears far more usually in the activities of life. Her union in the Osiris myth by no means blotted out her independent position and importance as a deity, though it gave her a far more widespread devotion. The union of Horus with the myth, and the establishment of Isis as the mother goddess, was the main mode of her importance in later times. Isis as the nursing mother is seldom shown until the twenty-sixth dynasty; then the type continually became more popular, until it outgrew all other religions of the country. In the Roman times the mother Isis not only received the devotion of all Egypt, but her worship spread rapidly abroad, like that of Mithra. It became the popular devotion of Italy; and, after a change of name due to the growth of Christianity, she has continued to receive the adoration of a large part of Europe down to the present day as the Madonna.

Nephthys - Neb-hat - was a shadowy double of Isis; reputedly her sister, and always associated with her, she seems to have no other function. Her name, "mistress of the palace," suggests that she was the consort of Osiris at the first, as a necessary but passive complement in the system of his kingdom. When the active Isis worship entered into the renovation of Osiris, Nebhat remained of nominal importance, but practically ignored.

Horus - Heru or Horu - has a more complex history than any other god. We cannot assign the various stages of it with certainty, but we can discriminate the following ideas:

(a) There was an elder or greater Horus, Hor-ur - or Aroeris of the Greeks - who was credited with being the brother of Osiris, older than Isis, Set, or Nephthys. He was always in human form, and was the god of Letopolis. This seems to have been the primitive god of a tribe cognate to the Osiris worshippers. What connection this god had with the hawk we do not know; often Horus is found written without the hawk, simply as hr, with the meaning of "upper" or "above." This word generally has the determinative of sky, and so means primitively the sky or one belonging to the sky. It is at least possible that there was a sky-god her at Letopolis, and likewise the hawk-god was a sky-god her at Edfu, and hence the mixture of the two deities.

(b) The hawk-god of the south, at Edfu and Hierakonpolis, became so firmly embedded in the myth as the avenger of Osiris, that we must accept the southern people as the ejectors of the Set tribe. It is always the hawk-headed Horus who wars against Set, and attends on the enthroned Osiris.

(c) The hawk Horus became identified with the sun-god, and hence came the winged solar disk as the emblem of Horus of Edfu, and the title of Horus on the horizons - at rising and setting - Hor-emakhti, Harmakhis of the Greeks.

(d) Another aspect resulting from Horus being the "sky" god, was that the sun and moon were his two eyes; hence he was Hor-merti, Horus of the two eyes; and the sacred eye of Horus - uza - became the most usual of all amulets.

(e) Horus, as conqueror of Set, appears as the hawk standing on the sign of gold, nub, nubti was the title of Set, and thus Horus is shown trampling upon Set; this became a usual title of the kings. There are many less important forms of Horus, but the form which outgrew all others in popular estimation was

(f) Hor-pe-khroti, Harpokrates of the Greeks, "Horus the child." As the son of Isis he constantly appears from the nineteenth dynasty onward. One of the earlier of these forms is that of the boy Horus standing upon crocodiles, and grasping scorpions and noxious animals in his hands. This type was a favorite amulet down to Ptolemaic times, and is often found carved in stone to be placed in a house, but was scarcely ever made in other materials or for suspension on the person, The form of the young Horus seated on an open lotus flower was also popular in the Greek times. But the infant Horus with his finger to his lips was the most popular form of all, sometimes alone, sometimes on his mother's lap. The finger, which pointed to his being a sucking child, was absurdly misunderstood by the Greeks as an emblem of silence. From the twenty-sixth dynasty down to late Roman times the infant Horus, or the young boy, was the most prominent subject on the temples, and the commonest figure in the homes of the people.

The other main group of human gods was Amon, Mut, and Khonsu of Thebes. Amon was the local god of Karnak, and owed his importance in Egypt to the political rise of his district. The Theban kingdom of the twelfth dynasty spread his fame, the great kings of the eighteenth and nineteenth dynasty ascribed their victories to Amon, his high priest became a political power which absorbed the state after the twentieth dynasty, and the importance of the god only ceased with the fall of his city. The original attributes and the origin of the name of Amon are unknown; but he became combined with Ra, the sun-god, and as Amon-Ra he was "king of the gods," and "lord of the thrones of the world." The supremacy of Amon was for some centuries an article of political faith, and many other gods were merged in him, and only survived as aspects of the great god of all. The queens were the high priestesses of the god, and he was the divine father of their children; the kings being only incarnations of Amon in their relation to the queens.

Mut, the great mother, was the goddess of Thebes, and hence the consort of Amon. She is often shown as leading and protecting the kings, and the queens appear in the character of this goddess. Little is known about her otherwise.

Khonsu is a youthful god combined in the Theban system as the son of Amon and Mut. He is closely parallel to Thôth as being a god of time, as a moon god, and of science, "the executor of plans." A large temple was dedicated to him at Karnak, but otherwise he was not of religious importance.

Neit was a goddess of the Libyan people; but her worship was firmly implanted by them in Egypt. She was a goddess of hunting and of weaving, the two arts of a nomadic people. Her emblem was a distaff with two crossed arrows, and her name was written with a figure of a weaver's shuttle. She was adored in the first dynasty, when the name Merneit, "loved by Neit," occurs; and her priesthood was one of the most usual in the pyramid period. She was almost lost to sight during some thousands of years, but she became the state goddess of the twenty-sixth dynasty, when the Libyans set up their capital in her city of Sais. In later times she again disappears from customary religion.

SUN AND SKY GODS

The gods which personify the sun and sky stand apart in their essential idea from those already described, although they were largely mixed and combined with other classes of gods. So much did this mixture pervade all the later views that some writers have seen nothing but varying forms of sun-worship in Egyptian religion. It will have been noticed however in the foregoing what a large body of theology was entirely apart from the sun-worship, while here we treat the latter as separate from the other elements with which it was more or less combined.

Ra was the great sun-god to whom every king pledged himself, by adopting on his accession a motto-title embodying the god's name such as Ra-men-kau,

"Ra established the kas"; Ra-sehotep-ab,

"Ra satisfied the heart"; Ra-neb-maat, "Ra is the lord of truth," and these titles were those by which the king was best known ever after. This devotion was not primitive, but began in the fourth dynasty, and was established by the fifth dynasty being called sons of Ra, and every later king having the title "son of Ra" before his name. The obelisk was the emblem of Ra, and in the fifth dynasty a great obelisk temple was built in his honor at Abusir, followed also by others. Heliopolis was the centre of his worship, where Senusert I, in the twelfth dynasty, rebuilt the temple and erected the obelisks, one of which is still standing. But Ra was preceded there by another sun-god, Atmu, who was the true god of the nome; and Ra, though worshipped throughout the land, was not the aboriginal god of any city. In Heliopolis he was attached to Atmu, at Thebes attached to Amen. These facts point to Ra having been introduced into Egypt by a conquering people, after the theologic settlement of the whole land. There are many suggestions that the Ra worshippers came in from Asia, and established their rule at Heliopolis. The title of the ruler of that place was the heq, a semitic title; and the heq sceptre was the sacred treasure of the temple. The "spirits of Heliopolis" were specially honored, an idea more Babylonian than Egyptian. This city was a centre of literary learning and of theologic theorizing which was unknown elsewhere in Egypt, but familiar in Mesopotamia. A conical stone was the embodiment of the god at Heliopolis, as in Syria. On, the native name of Heliopolis, occurs twice in Syria, as well as other cities named Heliopolis there in later times. The view of an early Semitic principate of Heliopolis, before the dynastic age, would unify all of these facts; and the advance of Ra worship in the fifth dynasty would be due to a revival of the influence of the eastern Delta at that time.

The form of Ra most free from admixture is that of the disk of the sun, sometimes figured between two hills at rising, sometimes between two wings, sometimes in the boat in which it floated on the celestial ocean across the sky. The winged disk has almost always two cobra serpents attached to it, and often two rams' horns; the meaning of the whole combination is that Ra protects and preserves, like the vulture brooding over its young, destroys like the cobra, and creates like the ram. This is seen by the modifications where it is placed over a king's head, when the destructive cobra is omitted, and the wings are folded together as embracing and protecting the king.

This disk form is connected with the hawk-god, by being placed over the head of the hawk; and this in turn is connected with the human form by the disk resting on the hawk-headed man, which is one of the most usual types of Ra. The god is but seldom shown as being purely human, except when identified with other gods, such as Atmu, Horus, or Amon.

The worship of Ra outshone all others in the nineteenth dynasty. United to the god of Thebes as Amon Ra, he became "king of the gods," and the view that the soul joined Ra in his journey through the hours of the night absorbed all other views, which only became sections of this whole. By the Greek times this belief seems to have practically given place to others, and it had practically vanished in the early Christian age.

Atmu (Tum) was the original god of Heliopolis and the Delta side, round to the gulf of Suez, which formerly reached up to Ismailiyeh. How far his nature as the setting sun was the result of his being identified with Ra, is not clear. It may The that the introduction of Ra led to his being unified with him. Those who take the view that the names of gods are connected with tribes, as Set and Suti, and Anak, might well claim that Atmu and Atum belonged to the land of Aduma or Etham.

Khepera has no local importance, but is named as the morning sun. He was worshipped about the time of the nineteenth dynasty.

Aten was a conception of the sun entirely different from Ra. No human or animal form was ever attached to it; and the adoration of the physical power and action of the sun was the sole devotion. So far as we can trace, it was a worship entirely apart and different from every other type of religion in Egypt; and the partial information that we have about it does not so far, show a single flaw in a purely scientific conception of the source of all life and power upon earth. The Aten was the only instance of a "jealous god" in Egypt, and this worship was exclusive of all others, and claims universality. There are traces of it shortly before Amenhotep III. He showed some devotion to it, and it was his son who took the name of Akhenaten, "the glory of the Aten," and tried to enforce this as the sole worship of Egypt. But it fell immediately after, and is lost in the next dynasty. The sun is represented as radiating its beams on all things, and every beam ends in a hand which imparts life and power to the king and to all else. In the hymn to the Aten the universal scope of this power is proclaimed as the source of all life and action, and every land and people are subject to it, and owe to it their existence and their allegiance. No such grand theology had ever appeared in the world before, so far as we know; and it is the forerunner of the later monotheist religions, while it is even more abstract and impersonal, and may well rank as a scientific theism.

Anher was the local god of Thinis in upper Egypt, and Sebennytos in the Delta a human sun-god. His name is a mere epithet, "he who goes in heaven"; and it may well be that this was only a title of Ra, who was thus worshipped at these places.

Sopdu was the god of the eastern desert, and he was identified with the cone of glowing zodiacal light which precedes the sunrise. His emblem was a mummified hawk, or a human figure.

Nut, the embodiment of heaven, is shown as a female figure dotted over with stars. She was not worshipped nor did she belong to any one place, but was a cosmogonic idea.

Seb, the embodiment of the earth, is figured as lying on the ground while Nut bends over him. He was the "prince of the gods," the power that went before all the later gods, the superseded Saturn of Egyptian theology. He is rarely mentioned, and no temples were dedicated to him, but he appears in the cosmic mythology. It seems, from their positions, that very possibly the Set and Nut were the primeval gods of the aborigines of Hottentot type, before the Osiris worshippers of European type ever entered the Nile Valley.

Shu was the god of space, who lifted up Nut from off the body of Seb. He was often represented, especially in late amulets; possibly it was believed that he would likewise raise up the body of the deceased from earth to heaven. His figure is entirely human, and he kneels on one knee with both hands lifted above his head. He was regarded as the father of Seb, the earth having been formed from space or chaos. His emblem was the ostrich feather, the lightest and most voluminous object.

Hapi, the Nile, must also be placed with nature-gods. He is figured as a man, or two men for the upper and lower Niles, holding a tray of produce of the land, and having large female breasts as being the nourisher of the valley. A favourite group consists of the two Nile figures tying the plants of upper and lower Egypt around the emblem of union. He was worshipped at Nilopolis, and also at the shrines which marked the boating stages, about a hundred in number, all along the river. Festivals were held at the rising of the Nile, like those still kept up at various stages of the inundation. Hymns in honor of the river attribute all prosperity and good to its benefits.

Ptah, the creator, was especially worshipped at. Memphis. He is figured as a mummy; and we know that full length burial and mummifying begin with the dynastic race. He was identified with the earlier animal-worship of the bull Apis; but it is not likely that this originated his creative aspect, as he creates by moulding clay, or by word and will, and not by natural means. He became united with the old Memphite god of the dead, Seker, and with Osiris, as Ptah-Seker-Osiris. Thus we learn that he belonged neither to the animal worshippers, the believers in Seker, nor to the Osiride race, but to a fourth people.

Min was the male principle. He was worshipped mainly at Ekhmim and Koptos, and was there identified with Pan by the Greeks. He also was the god of the desert, out to the Red Sea. The oldest statues of gods are three gigantic limestone figures of Min found at Koptos; these bear relief designs of Red Sea shells and swordfish. It seems, then, that he was introduced by a people coming across from the east. His worship continued till Roman times.

Hathor was the female principle whose animal was the cow; and she is identified with the mother Isis. She was also identified with other earlier deities; and her forms are very numerous in different localities. There were also seven Hathors who appear as fates, presiding over birth.

Footnotes
3. For instance the words sek, to move; seg, to go; sek, to destroy.

CHAPTER III

THE PTAH-HOTEP AND THE KE'GEMNI:
THE OLDEST BOOKS IN THE WORLD

The Instructions of Ptah-hotep and of Ke'gemni possess, apart from the curious nature of their contents, a feature of the greatest interest, and an adequate claim on the notice of all persons interested in literature and its history. For if the datings and ascriptions in them be accepted as trustworthy - there is no reason why they should not be accepted - they were composed about four thousand years before Christ, and three thousand five hundred and fifty years before Christ, respectively. And the significance of those remote dates is, that they are the oldest books in the world, the earliest extant specimens of the literary art. They stand on the extreme horizon of all that ocean of paper and ink that has become to us as an atmosphere, a fifth element, an essential of life.

Books of many kinds had of course been written for centuries before Ptah-hotep of Memphis summarised, for the benefit of future generations, the leading principles of morality current in his day; even before the Vizier, five hundred years earlier, gave to his children the scroll which they prized above all things on earth;[4] but those have perished and these remain. There are lists of titles which have a large sound, and prayers to the gods for all good things, on the tombs and monuments of kings and magnates long before the time Ke'gemni; but those are not books in any sense of that word. Even the long, strange chants and spells engraven in the royal pyramids over against Memphis are later than the time of Ptah-hotep, and cannot be called books in their present form, although some of them apparently originated before the First Dynasty.[5]

Nor do the oldest books of any other country approach these two in antiquity. To draw comparisons between them let us, in imagination, place ourselves at the period at which Ptah-hotep lived, that is about B.C. 3550, "under King Isosi, living forever," and take a glance at futurity.

The Babylonians are doubtless exercising their literary talents; but they will leave nothing worthy the name of book to the far posterity of fifty-four centuries hence. Thirteen centuries shall pass before Hammurabi, King of Babylon, drafts the code of laws that will be found at that time. Only after two thousand years shall Moses write on the origin of things, and the Vedas be arranged in their present form. It will be two-and-a-half thousand years before the Great King of Jerusalem will set in order many proverbs and write books so much resembling, in form and style, that of Ptah-hotep; before the source and summit of European literature will write his world epics. For the space of years between Solomon and ourselves, great though it seem, is not so great as that between Solomon and Ptah-hotep.

Nothing definite is known concerning these two nobles beyond what is said of them in their works. A fine tomb of a certain Ke'gemni exists at Memphis; his titles, so far as can be ascertained, are: Judge of the High Court; Governor of the Land unto its Limit, South and North; Director of every Command. He has sometimes been supposed to be identical with our Ke'gemni; but I am assured by those most competent to judge that this tomb cannot be earlier than the fifth dynasty, - a good three hundred years from the date assigned to the moralist, - so that the theory that they are one person may be dismissed as highly improbable. No other person of the name is known.

The position is much the same with Ptah-hotep. There are near Memphis the tombs of several nobles of this name, of whom two lived in the reign of Isosi; and in this case, again, it has been assumed that one of these two must be the writer of the Instruction. But in neither instance do the titles coincide with or include those assigned to him. The highest title which he bears, Eldest Son of the King, does not anywhere appear in these tombs. It is true that one of these contemporaries was hereditary chief; but we know that Ptah-hotep was a common name at this time, and in the absence of more certain proof it will be well to abstain from the identification of like names upon insufficient grounds.

THE INSTRUCTION OF PTAH-HOTEP (THE GOD PTAH IS SATISFIED)

The Instruction of the Governor of his City, the Vizier, Ptah-hotep, in the Reign of King of Upper and Lower Egypt, Isosi, living forever, to the end of Time.

A. The Governor of his City, the Vizier, Ptah-hotep, he said: "O Prince my Lord, the end of life is at hand; old age descendeth - upon me - ; feebleness cometh, and childishness is renewed. He - that is old - lieth down in misery every day. The eyes are small; the ears are deaf. Energy is diminished, the heart hath no rest. The mouth is silent, and he speaketh no word; the heart stoppeth, and he remembereth not yesterday. The bones are painful throughout the body; good turneth into evil. All taste departeth. These things doeth old age for mankind, being evil in all things. The nose is stopped, and he breatheth not for weakness (?), whether standing or sitting.

"Command thy servant, therefore, to make over my, princely authority - to my son - . Let me speak unto him the words of them that hearken to the counsel of the men of old time; those that once hearkened unto the gods. I pray thee, let this thing be done, that sin may be banished from among persons of understanding, that thou may enlighten the lands."

Said the Majesty of this God: [6] "Instruct him, then, in the words of old time; may he be a wonder unto the children of princes, that they may enter and hearken with him. Make straight all their hearts; and discourse with him, without causing weariness."

B. Here begin the proverbs of fair speech, spoken by the Hereditary Chief, the Holy Father, Beloved of the God, the Eldest Son of the King, of his body, the

Governor of his City, the Vizier, Ptah-hotep, when instructing the ignorant in the knowledge of exactness in fair speaking; the glory of him that obeyeth, the shame of him that transgresseth them. He said unto his son:

1. Be not proud because thou art learned; but discourse with the ignorant man, as with the sage. For no limit can be set to skill, neither is there any craftsman that possesseth full advantages. Fair speech is more rare than the emerald that is found by slave-maidens on the pebbles.

2. If thou find an arguer talking, one that is well disposed and wiser than thou, let thine arms fall, bend thy back,[7] be not angry with him if he agree (?) not with thee. Refrain from speaking evilly; oppose him not at any time when he speaketh. If he address thee as one ignorant of the matter, thine humbleness shall bear away his contentions.

3. If thou find an arguer talking, thy fellow, one that is within thy reach, keep not silence when he saith aught that is evil; so shalt thou be wiser than he. Great will be the applause on the part of the listeners, and thy name shall be good in the knowledge of princes.

4. If thou find an arguer talking, a poor man, that is to say not thine equal, be not scornful toward him because he is lowly. Let him alone; then shall he confound himself. Question him not to please thine heart, neither pour out thy wrath upon him that is before thee; it is shameful to confuse a mean mind. If thou be about to do that which is in thine heart, overcome it as a thing rejected of princes.

5. If thou be a leader, as one directing the conduct of the multitude, endeavor always to be gracious, that thine own conduct be without defect. Great is Truth, appointing a straight path; never hath it been overthrown since the reign of Osiris.[8] One that oversteppeth the laws shall be punished. Overstepping is by the covetous man; but degradations (?) bear off his riches. Never hath evil-doing, brought its venture safe to port. For he saith, "I will obtain by myself for myself," and saith not, "I will obtain because I am allowed." But the limits of justice are steadfast; it is that which a man repeateth from his father.

6. Cause not fear among men; for - this - the God punisheth likewise. For there is a man that saith, "Therein is life"; and he is bereft of the bread of his mouth. There is a man that saith, "Power - is therein"; and he saith, "I seize for myself that which I perceive." Thus a man speaketh, and he is smitten down. It is another that attaineth by giving unto him that hath not. Never hath that which men have prepared for come to pass; for what the God hath commanded, even that thing cometh to pass. Live, therefore, in the house of kindliness, and men shall come and give gifts of themselves.

7. If thou be among the guests of a man that is greater than thou, accept that which he giveth thee, putting it to thy lips. If thou look at him that is before thee - thine host - pierce him not with many glances. It is abhorred of the soul[9] to stare at him. Speak not until he address thee; one knoweth not what may be evil in

his opinion. Speak when he questioneth thee; so shall thy speech be good in his opinion. The noble who sitteth before food divideth it as his soul moveth him; he giveth unto him that he would favour - it is the custom of the evening meal. It is his soul that guideth his hand. It is the noble that bestoweth, not the underling that attaineth. Thus the eating of bread is under the providence of the God; he is an ignorant man that disputeth it.

8. If thou be an emissary sent from one noble to another, be exact after the manner of him that sent thee, give his message even as he hath said it. Beware of making enmity by thy words, setting one noble against the other by perverting truth. Overstep it not, neither repeat that which any man, be he prince or peasant, saith in opening the heart; it is abhorrent to the soul.

9. If thou have ploughed, gather thine harvest in the field, and the God shall make it great under thine hand. Fill not thy mouth at any neighbor's table . . . [10] If a crafty man be the possessor of wealth, he stealeth like a crocodile from the priests.

Let not a man be envious that hath no children; let him be neither downcast nor quarrelsome on account of it. For a father, though great, may be grieved; as to the mother of children, she hath less peace than another. Verily, each man is created - to his destiny - by the God, who is the chief of a tribe, trustful in following him.

10. If thou be lowly, serve a wise man, that all thine actions may be good before the God. If thou have known a man of none account that hath been advanced in rank, be not haughty toward him on account of that which thou knowest concerning him; but honour him that hath been advanced, according to that which he hath become.

Behold, riches come not of themselves; it is their rule for him that desireth them. If he bestir him and collect them himself, the God shall make him prosperous; but He shall punish him, if he be slothful.

11. Follow thine heart during thy lifetime; do not more than is commanded thee. Diminish not the time of following the heart; it is abhorred of the soul, that its time - of ease - be taken away. Shorten not the daytime more than is needful to maintain thy house. When riches are gained, follow the heart; for riches are of no avail if one be weary.

12. If thou wouldest be a wise man, beget a son for the pleasing of the God. If he make straight his course after thine example, if he arrange thine affairs in due order, do unto him all that is good, for thy son is he, begotten of thine own soul. Sunder not thine heart from him, or thine own begotten shall curse - thee - . If he be heedless and trespass thy rules of conduct, and is violent; if every speech that cometh from his mouth be a vile word; then beat thou him, that his talk may be fitting. Keep him from those that make light of that which is commanded, for it is they that make him rebellious. And they that are guided go not astray, but they that lose their bearings cannot find a straight course.

13. If thou be in the chamber of council, act always according to the steps enjoined on thee at the beginning of the day. Be not absent, or thou shalt be expelled; but be ready in entering and making report. Wide [11] is the seat of one that hath made address. The council chamber acteth by strict rule; and all its plans are in accordance with method. It is the God that advanceth one to a seat therein; the like is not done for elbowers.

14. If thou be among people, make for thyself love, the beginning and end of the heart. One that knoweth not his course shall say in himself - seeing thee - , "He that ordereth himself duly becometh the owner of wealth; I shall copy his conduct." Thy name shall be good, though thou speak not; thy body shall be fed; thy face shall be - seen - among thy neighbors; thou shalt be provided with what thou lackest. As to the man whose heart obeyeth his belly, he causeth disgust in place of love. His heart is wretched (?), his body is gross (?), he is insolent toward those endowed of the God. He that obeyeth his belly hath an enemy. [12]

15. Report thine actions without concealment; discover thy conduct when in council with thine overlord. It is not evil for the envoy that his report be not answered. "Yea, I know it," by the prince; for that which he knoweth includeth not - this. If he - the prince - think that he will oppose him on account of it, - he thinketh - "He will be silent because I have spoken." [13]

16. If thou be a leader, cause that the rules that thou hast enjoined be carried out; and do all things as one that remembereth the days coming after, when speech availeth not. Be not lavish of favours; it leadeth to servility (?), producing slackness.

17. If thou be a leader, be gracious when thou hearkenest unto the speech of a suppliant. Let him not hesitate to deliver himself of that which he hath thought to tell thee; but be desirous of removing his injury. Let him speak freely, that the thing for which he hath come to thee may be done. If he hesitate to open his heart, it is said, "Is it because he - the judge - doeth the wrong that no entreaties are made to him concerning it by those to whom it happeneth?" But a well taught heart hearkeneth readily.

18. If thou desire to continue friendship in any abode wherein thou interest, be it as master, as brother, or as friend; wheresoever thou goest, beware of consorting with women. No place prospereth wherein that is done. Nor is it prudent to take part in it; a thousand men have been ruined for the pleasure of a little time short as a dream. Even death is reached thereby; it is a wretched thing. As for the evil liver, one leaveth him for what he doeth, he is avoided. If his desires be not gratified, he regardeth (?) no laws.

19. If thou desire that thine actions may be good, save thyself from all malice, and beware of the quality of covetousness, which is a grievous inner (?) Malady. Let it not chance that thou fall thereinto. It setteth at variance fathers-in-law and the kinsmen of the daughter-in-law; it sundereth the wife and the husband. It gathereth unto itself all evils; it is the girdle of all wickedness.[14] But the man that

is just flourisheth; truth goes in his footsteps, and he maketh habitations therein, not in the dwelling of covetousness.

20. Be not covetous as touching shares, in seizing that which is not thine own property. Be not covetous toward thy neighbors; for with a gentleman praise availeth more than might. He - that is covetous - cometh empty from among his neighbours, being void of the persuasion of speech. One hath remorse for even a little covetousness when his belly cooleth.

21. If thou wouldest be wise, provide for thine house, and love thy wife that is in thine arms. Fill her stomach, clothe her back; oil is the remedy of her limbs. Gladden her heart during thy lifetime, for she is an estate profitable unto its lord. Be not harsh, for gentleness mastereth her more than strength. Give (?) to her that for which she sigheth and that toward which her eye looketh; so shall thou keep her in thy house. . . .

22. Satisfy thine hired servants out of such things as thou hast; it is the duty of one that hath been favoured of the God. In sooth, it is hard to satisfy hired servants. For one[15] saith, 'He is a lavish person; one knoweth not that which may come - from him." But on the morrow he thinketh, 'We is a person of exactitude - parsimony - content therein." And when favours have been shown unto servants, they say, "We go." Peace dwelleth not in that town wherein dwell servants that are wretched.

23. Repeat not extravagant speech, neither listen thereto; for it is the utterance of a body heated by wrath. When such speech is repeated to thee, hearken not thereto, look to the ground. Speak not regarding it, that he that is before thee may know wisdom. If thou be commanded to do a theft, bring it to pass that the command be taken off thee, for it is a thing hateful according to law. That which destroyeth a vision is the veil over it.

24. If thou wouldest be a wise man, and one sitting in council with his overlord, apply thine heart unto perfection. Silence is more profitable unto thee than abundance of speech. Consider how thou may be opposed by an expert that speaketh in council. It is a foolish thing to speak on every kind of work, for he that disputeth thy words shall put them unto proof.

25. If thou be powerful, make thyself to be honoured for knowledge and for gentleness. Speak with authority, that is, not as if following injunctions, for he that is humble - when highly placed - falleth into errors. Exalt not thine heart, that it be not brought low. Be not silent, but beware of interruption and of answering words with heat. Put it far from thee; control thyself. The wrathful heart speaketh fiery words; it darteth out at the man of peace that approacheth, stopping his path.

One that reckoneth accounts all the day passeth not an happy moment. One that gladdeneth his heart all the day provideth not for his house. The bowman hitteth the mark, as the steersman reacheth land, by diversity of aim. He that obeyeth his heart shall command.[16]

26. Let not a prince be hindered when he is occupied; neither oppress the

heart of him that is already laden. For he shall be hostile toward one that delayeth him, but shall bare his soul unto one that loveth him. The disposal of souls is with the God, and that which He loveth is His creation. Set out, therefore, after a violent quarrel; be at peace with him that is hostile unto - thee - his opponent. It is such souls that make love to grow.

27. Instruct a noble in such things as be profitable unto him; cause that he be received among men. Let his satisfaction fall on his master, for thy provision dependeth upon his will. By reason of it thy belly shall be satisfied; thy back will be clothed thereby. Let him receive thine heart, that thine house may flourish and thine honour - if thou wish it to flourish - thereby. He shall extend thee a kindly hand. Further, he shall implant the love of thee in the bodies of thy friends. Forsooth, it is a soul loving to hearken. [17]

28. If thou be the son of a man of the priesthood, and an envoy to conciliate the multitude. . . . [18] speak thou without favouring one side. Let it not be said: "His conduct is that of the nobles, favouring one side in his speech." Turn thine aim toward exact judgments.

29. If thou have been gracious at a former time, having forgiven a man to guide him aright, shun him, remind him not after the first day that he hath been silent to thee - -concerning it.

30. If thou be great, after being of none account, and hast gotten riches after squalour, being foremost in these in the city, and hast knowledge concerning useful matters, so that promotion is come unto thee; then swathe not thine heart in thine hoard, for thou art become the steward of the endowments of the God. Thou art not the last; another shall be thine equal, and to him shall come the like-fortune and station.

31. Bend thy back unto thy chief, thine overseer in the King's palace, for thine house dependeth upon his wealth, and thy wages in their season. How foolish is one that quarrelleth with his chief, for one liveth only while he is gracious. . . .

Plunder not the houses of tenants; neither steal the things of a friend, lest he accuse thee in thine bearing, which thrusteth back the heart.[19] If he know of it, he will do thee an injury. Quarrelling in place of friendship is a foolish thing.

32. - Concerning unnatural sin.

33. If thou wouldest seek out the nature of a friend, ask it not of any companion of his; but pass a time with him alone, that thou injure not his affairs. Debate with him after a season; test his heart in an occasion of speech. When he hath told thee his past life, he hath made an opportunity that thou may either be ashamed for him or be familiar with him. Be not reserved with him when he openeth speech, neither answer him after a scornful manner. Withdraw not thyself from him, neither interrupt (?) him whose matter is not yet ended, whom it is possible to benefit.

34. Let thy face be bright what time thou livest. That which goeth into the

storehouse must come out therefrom; and bread is to be shared. He that is grasping in entertainment shall himself have an empty belly; he that causeth strife cometh himself to sorrow. Take not such an one for thy companion. It is a man's kindly acts that are remembered of him in the years after his life.[20]

35. Know well thy merchants; for when thine affairs are in evil case, thy good repute among thy friends is a channel (?) which is filled. It is more important than the dignities of a man; and the wealth of one passeth to another. The good repute of a man's son is a glory unto him; and a good character is for remembrance.

36. Correct chiefly; instruct conformably - therewith. Vice must be drawn out that virtue may remain. Nor is this a matter of misfortune, for one that is a gainsayer becometh a strifemaker.

37. If thou make a woman to be ashamed, wanton of heart, not known by her townfolk, to be falsely placed, be kind unto her for a space, send her not away, give her to eat. The wantonness of her heart shall esteem thy guidance.

C. If thou obey these things that I have said unto thee, all thy demeanour shall be of the best; for verily, the quality of truth is among their excellences. Set the memory of them in the mouths of the people; for their proverbs are good. Nor shall any word that hath here been set down cease out of this land for ever, but shall be made a pattern whereby princes shall speak well. They - my words - shall instruct a man how he shall speak, after he hath heard them; yea, he shall become as one skillful in obeying, excellent in speaking, after he hath heard them. Good fortune shall befall him, for he shall be of the highest rank. He shall be gracious to the end of his life; he shall be contented always. His knowledge shall be his guide (?) into a place of security, wherein he shall prosper while on earth. The scholar [21] shall be content in his knowledge. As to the prince, in his turn, forsooth, his heart shall be happy, his tongue made straight. And - in these proverbs - his lips shall speak, his eyes shall see, and his ears shall hear, that which is profitable for his son, so that he deal justly, void of deceit.

38. A splendid thing is the obedience of an obedient son; he cometh in and listeneth obediently.

Excellent in hearing, excellent in speaking, is every man that obeyeth what is noble, and the obedience of an obeyer is a noble thing.

Obedience is better than all things that are; it maketh good-will.

How good it is that a son should take that from his father by which he hath reached old age - obedience.

That which is desired by the God is obedience; disobedience is abhorred of the God.

Verily, it is the heart that maketh its master to obey or to disobey; for the safe and sound life of a man are his heart.

It is the obedient man that obeyeth what is said; he that loveth to obey, the same shall carry out commands.

He that obeyeth becometh one obeyed.

It is good indeed when a son obeyeth his father; and he-his father-that hath spoken hath great joy of it. Such a son shall be mild as a master, and he that heareth him shall obey him that hath spoken. He shall be comely in body and honoured by his father. His memory shall be in the mouths of the living, those upon earth, as long as they exist.[22]

39. Let a son receive the word of his father, not being heedless of any rule of his. Instruct thy son - thus; - for the obedient man is one that is perfect in the opinion of princes. If he direct his mouth by what hath been enjoined him. watchful and obedient, thy son shall be wise, and his going seemly. Heedlessness leadeth into disobedience on the morrow; but understanding shall establish him. As for the fool, he shall be crushed.

40. As for the fool, devoid of obedience, he doeth nothing. Knowledge he regardeth as ignorance. profitable things are hurtful things. He doeth all kinds of errors, so that he is rebuked therefor every day. He liveth in death therewith; it is his food. At chattering speech he marvelleth, as at the wisdom of princes, living in death every day. He is shunned because of his misfortunes, by reason of the multitude of afflictions that cometh upon]him every day.

41. A son that hearkeneth is as a Follower of Horus.[23] He is good after he hearkeneth; he groweth old, he reacheth honour and reverence. He repeated in like manner to his sons and daughters, so renewing the instruction of his father. Each man instructeth as did his begetter, repeating it unto his children. Let them - in turn - speak with their sons and daughters, that they may be famous in their deeds. Let that which thou speaketh implant true things and just in the life of thy children. Then the highest authority shall arrive, and sins depart - from them. And such men as see these things shall say, "Surely that man hath spoken to good purpose," and they shall do likewise; or, "But surely that man was experienced." And all people shall declare, "It is they that shall direct the multitude; dignities are not complete without them."

Take not my word away, neither add one; set not one in the place of another. Beware of opening . . .[24] in thyself.

Be wary of speech when a learned man hearkeneth unto thee; desire to be established for good in the mouth of those that hear thee speaking. If thou have entered as an expert, speak with exact (?) lips, that thy conduct may be seemly.

42. Be thine heart overflowing; but refrain thy mouth. Let thy conduct be exact while amongst nobles, and seemly before thy lord, doing that which he hath commanded. Such a son shall speak unto them that hearken to him; moreover, his begetter shall be favoured. Apply thine heart, what time thou speakest, to saying things such that the nobles who listen declare, "How excellent is that which cometh out of his mouth!"

43. Carry out the behest of thy lord to thee. How good is the teaching of a man's father, for he hath come from him, who hath spoken of his son while he was yet unborn; and that which is done for him - the son - is more than that which

is commanded him. Forsooth, a good son is of the gift of the God; he doeth more than is enjoined on him, he doeth right, and putteth his heart into all his goings.

D. If now thou attain thy position, the body shall flourish, the King shall be content in all that thou doest, and thou shalt gather years of life not fewer than I have passed upon earth. I have gathered even fivescore and ten years of life, for the King hath bestowed upon me favours more than upon my forefathers; this because I wrought truth and justice for the King unto mine old age.

It Is Finished
From Its Beginning To Its End
Even As Found In Writing.

THE INSTRUCTION OF KE'GEMNI (KE'GEMNI - I HAVE FOUND A SOUL)

1. The cautious man flourisheth, the exact one is praised; the innermost chamber openeth unto the man of silence. Wide [25] is the seat of the man gentle of speech; but knives are prepared against one that forceth a path, that he advance not, save in due season.

2. If thou sit with a company of people, desire not the bread that thou likest; short is the time of restraining the heart, and gluttony is an abomination; therein is the quality of a beast. A handful of water quencheth the thirst, and a mouthful of melon supporteth the heart. A good thing standeth for goodness, but some small thing standeth for plenty.[26] A base man is he that is governed by his belly; he departeth only when he is no longer able to fill full his belly in men's houses.

3. If thou sit with a glutton, eat with him, then depart (?).

If thou drink with a drunkard, accept - drink - and his heart shall be satisfied.

Refuse not meat when with a greedy man. Take that which he giveth thee; set it not on one side, thinking that it will be a courteous thing.

4. If a man be lacking in good fellowship, no speech hath any influence over him. He is sour of face toward the glad-hearted that are kindly to him; he is a grief unto his mother and his friends; and all men - cry - , "Let thy name be known; thou art silent in thy mouth when thou art addressed!"

5. Be not haughty because of thy might in the midst of thy young soldiers. Beware of making strife, for one knoweth not the things that the God will do when He punisheth.

The Vizier caused his sons and daughters to be summoned, when he had finished the rules of the conduct of men. And they marvelled when they came to him. Then he said unto them, "Hearken unto everything that is in writing in this book, even as I have said it in adding unto profitable sayings." And they cast themselves on their bellies, and they read it, even as it was in writing. And it was better in their opinion than anything in this land unto its limits.

Now they were living when His Majesty, the King of upper and lower Egypt, Heuni, departed, and His Majesty, the King of upper and lower Egypt, Senforu, was enthroned as a gracious king over the whole of this land.

Then was Ke'gemni made Governor of his city and Vizier.

THE INSTRUCTIONS OF AMENEMHE'ET (THE GOD AMON IS FIRST)

Beginneth here the Instruction made by the majesty of the King of upper and lower Egypt, Sehotep'eb-Re, son of the Sun, Amenemhe'et, the Justified.[27] He speaketh thus in discovering words of truth unto his son, the Lord of the World:

1. Shine forth, he saith, even as the God. Hearken to that which I say unto thee; that thou may reign over the land, that thou may govern the world, that thou may excel in goodness.

2. Let one withdraw himself from his subordinates entirely. It befalleth that mankind give their hearts unto one that causeth them fear. Mix not among them alone; fill not thine heart with a brother; know not a trusted friend; make for thyself no familiar dependents; in these things is no satisfaction.

3. When thou liest down have a care for thy [28] very life, since friends exist not for a man in the day of misfortunes. I gave to the beggar, and caused the orphan to live; I made him that had not to attain, even as he that had.

4. But it was the eater of my food that made insurrection against me; to whom I gave mine hands, he created disturbance thereby; they that arrayed them in my fine linen regarded me as a shadow; and it was they that anointed themselves with my spices that entered my harem.

5. My images are among the living; and my achievements are among men. But I have made an heroic story that hath not been heard; a great feat of arms that hath not been seen. Surely one fighteth for a lassoed ox that forgetteth yesterday;[29] and good fortune is of no avail unto one that cannot perceive it.

6. It was after the evening meal, and night was come. I took for myself an hour of ease. I lay down upon my bed, for I was weary. My heart began to wander (?). I slept. And lo! weapons were brandished, and there was conference concerning me. I acted as the serpent of the desert.[30]

7. I awoke to fight; I was alone. I found one struck down, it was the captain of the guard. Had I received quickly the arms from his hand, I had driven back the dastards by smiting around. But he was not a brave man on that night, nor could I fight alone; an occasion of prowess cometh not to one surprised. Thus was I.

8. Behold, then, vile things came to pass, for I was without thee; the courtiers knew not that I had passed on to thee - my power. I sat not with thee on the throne.[31] Let me then, make my plans. Because I awed them not I was not unmindful of them; but mine heart bringeth not to remembrance the slackness of servants.

9. Have ever women gathered together assailants? Are assassins reared within my palace? Was the opening done by cutting through the ground? The underlings were deceived as to what they did.[32] But misfortunes have not come in my train since my birth; nor hath there existed the equal of me as a doer of valiance.

10. I forced my way up to Elephantine, I went down unto the coast-lakes;[33] I have stood upon the boundaries of the land, and I have seen its centre. I have set the limits of might by my might in my deeds.

11. I raised corn, I loved Nopi;[34] the Nile begged of me every valley. In my reign none hungered; none thirsted therein. They were contented in that which I did, saying concerning me, "Every commandment is meet."

12. I overcame lions; I carried off crocodiles. I cast the Nubians under my feet; I carried off the southern Nubians; I caused the Asiatics to flee, even as hounds.

13. I have made me an house, adorned with gold, its ceilings with lapis lazuli, its walls having deep foundations. Its doors are of copper, their bolts are of bronze. It is made for everlasting; eternity is in awe of it. I know every dimension thereof, O Lord of the World!

14. There are divers devices in buildings. I know the pronouncements of men when inquiring into its beauties; but they know not that it was without thee, O my Son, Senwesert; life, safe and sound, be to thee - by thy feet do I walk; thou art after mine own heart; by thine eyes do I see; born in an hour of delight; with spirits[35] that rendered thee praise.

15. Behold, that which I have done at the beginning, let me set it in order for thee at the end; let me be the landing-place of that which is in thine heart. All men together set the White Crown on the Offspring of the God. fixing it unto its due place. I shall begin thy praises when in the Boat of Ra. Thy kingdom hath been from primeval time; not by my doing, who have done valiant things. Raise up monuments, make beautiful thy tomb. I have fought against him whom thou knowest; for I desire not that he should be beside thy Majesty. Life safe and sound, be to thee.

Footnotes
4. The monuments leave no doubt of this. Pen and ink were used in the First Dynasty, and speech had been reduced to visible signs before that.
5. About B.C. 4770. In all Egyptian dates given in this book I follow Professor Petrie's chronology.
6. The King.
7. The customary attitude of a submissive inferior at that time.
8. The god Osiris was believed to have reigned on earth many thousand years before Menes, the first historical king.
9. soul - Ka'.
10. An obscure or corrupt phrase here follows, which does not admit of satisfactory translation.
11. I.e., comfortable.
12. His belly, presumably.
13. The above translation is not satisfactory; the text may be corrupt. No intelligible translation of it has yet been made.

14. I.e.., all wickedness is contained therein.

15. A servant.

16. So also in life, by diversity of aim, alternating work and play, happiness is secured. Tacking is evidently meant in the case of the steersman.

17. This section refers to the relations between the son of a nobleman and his tutor, dwelling on the benefits from former pupils in high places, if their school days have been pleasant.

18. An obscure phrase.

19. Literally, "It is that which preventeth the heart from advancing (?)" A curious phrase.

20. Literally, after his stick or sceptre.

21. Who knows them.

22. The greater part of this section is a play upon the root sodem, which in its meaning includes our hear - listen - and obey. This tiresome torture of words is frequent in Egyptian, especially in old religious texts.

23. The "Followers of Horns" are a legendary dynasty of demigods, believed by the Egyptians to have ruled for about 13,400 years after the reign of Horus, and before that of Menes. There is also an order of spirits by this name.

24. A word of unknown meaning; apparently some kind of plant. Such a word seems out of place here, and may be idiomatic, like our "flowery language." But the preceding line obviously refers to this book.

25. Comfortable.

26. This is a rather dark saying, but apparently the author means that although the duly instructed guest may only partake moderately of the abundance before him, what he cats is as good as the rest. His portion will be equal to the whole as regards quality, though inferior as regards quantity.

27. A ceremonial title applied to deceased persons, analogous to our "the late." "Justified" is not an exact rendering, but it is usual, and will serve.

28. Literally, heart.

29. An allusion to the people of Egypt, whom he had freed from the foreign oppressors.

30. He remained quiet but watchful.

31. Referring to the co-regency with his son.

32. Referring to the attempted assassination.

33. The limits, south and north, of his Kingdom.

34. The god of corn.

35. Or, unborn souls.

CHAPTER IV

THE "BOOK OF THE DEAD"

The Book of the Dead, the Egyptian title of which, "Pert em hru," has been variously translated "coming forth by day" and the "manifestation day," is a great body of religious compositions compiled for the use of the dead in the other world. It is probable that the name had a significance for the Egyptians which is incapable of being rendered in any modern language, and is borne out by another of its titles - "The chapter of making perfect the Khu" - or spirit. Texts dealing with the welfare of the dead and their life in the world beyond the grave are known to have been in use among the Egyptians as early as 4000 B.C. The oldest form of the Book of the Dead known to us is represented in the Pyramid Texts. With the invention of mummification a more complete funerary ritual arose, based on the hope that such ceremonies as it imposed would ensure the corpse against corruption, preserve it forever, and introduce it to a beatified existence among the gods. Almost immediately prior to the dynastic era a great stimulus appears to have been given to the cult of Osiris throughout Egypt. He had now become the god of the dead par excellence, and his dogma taught that from the preserved corpse would spring a beautiful astral body, the future home of the spirit of the deceased. It therefore became necessary to adopt measures of the greatest precaution for the preservation of human remains.

The generality of the texts comprised in the "'Book of the Dead" are in one form or another of much greater antiquity than the period of Mena, the first historical king of Egypt. Indeed, from internal evidence it is possible to show that many of these were revised or edited long before the copies known to us were made. Even at as early a date as 3300 B.C., the professional writers who transcribed the ancient texts appear to have been so puzzled by their contents that they hardly understood their purport. Dr. Budge states: "We are in any case justified in estimating the earliest form of the work to be contemporaneous with the foundation of the civilization which we call 'Egyptian' in the Valley of the Nile."

A "DISCOVERY" 3400 YEARS OLD

A hieratic inscription upon the sarcophagus of Queen Khnem-nefert, wife of Mentu-hetep, a king of the eleventh dynasty, c.2500 B.C., states that a certain chapter of the Book of the Dead was discovered in the reign of Hesep-ti, the fifth king of the first dynasty, who flourished about 4266 B.C. This sarcophagus affords us two copies of the said chapter, one immediately following the other. That as early as 2500 B.C., a chapter of the Book of the Dead should be referred to a date almost 2000 years before that time is astounding, and the mind reels before the idea of a tradition which, during comparatively unlettered centuries, could have conserved a religious formula almost unimpaired. Thus thirty-four centuries ago a portion of the Book of the Dead was regarded as extremely ancient, mysterious, and difficult of comprehension. It will be noted also that the inscription on the tomb of Queen Khnem-nefert bears out that the chapter in question was "discovered" about 4266 B.C. If it were merely discovered at that early era, what periods of remoteness lie between that epoch and the time when it was first reduced to writing? The description of the chapter on the sarcophagus of the royal lady states that "this chapter was found in the foundations beneath the Dweller in the Hennu Boat by the foreman of the builders in the time of the king of the South and North, Hesep-ti, whose word is truth"; and the Nebseni Papyrus says that the chapter was found in the city of Khemennu, or Hermopolis, on a block of alabaster, written in letters of lapis-lazuli, under the feet of the god. It also appears from the Turin Papyrus, which dates from the period of the twenty-sixth dynasty, that the name of the finder was Heru-ta-ta-f, the son of Cheops, who was at the time engaged in a tour of inspection of the temples. Sir Gaston Maspero is doubtful concerning the importance which should be attached to the statement regarding the chapter on the tomb of Queen Khnem-nefert, but M. Naville considers the chapter in question one of the oldest in the Book of the Dead.

A bas-relief of the second dynasty bears an inscription dedicating to the shade of a certain priest the formula of the "thousand loaves of bread, thousands of jugs of ale," and so forth, so common in later times. We thus see that 4000 years B.C. it was regarded as a religious duty to provide offerings of meat and drink for the dead, and there seems to be good evidence, from the nature of the formula in question, that it had become fixed and ritualistic by this period. This passage would appear to justify the text of the sarcophagus of the wife of Mentu-hetep. A few centuries later, about the time of Seneferu, c. 3766 B.C., the cult of the dead had expanded greatly from the architectural point of view, and larger and more imposing cenotaphs were provided for them. Victorious wars had brought much wealth to Egypt, and its inhabitants were better able to meet the very considerable expenditure entailed upon them by one of the most expensive cults known to the history of religion. In the reign of Men-kau-Ra a revision of certain parts of the text of the Book of the Dead appears to have been undertaken. The authority for this is the rubrics attached to certain chapters which state that they were found inscribed upon a block of alabaster in letters of lapis-lazuli in the time of that monarch.

We do not find a text comprising the Book of the Dead as a whole until the reign of Unas, 3333 B.C., whose pyramid was opened in 1881 by Sir G. Maspero. The stone walls were covered with texts extremely difficult of decipherment, because of their archaic character and spelling, among them many from the Book of the Dead. Continuing his excavations at Saqqarah, Maspero made his way into the pyramid of Teta, 3300 B.C., in which he discovered inscriptions, some of which were identical with those in the pyramid of Unas, so that the existence of a fully formed Book of the Dead by the time of the first king of the sixth dynasty was proven. Additional texts were found in the tomb of Pepi I, 3233 B.C. From this it will be seen that before the close of the sixth dynasty five copies of a series of texts, forming the Book of the Dead of that period, are in evidence, and, as has been observed, there is substantial proof that its ceremonial was in vogue in the second, and probably in the first, dynasty. Its texts continued to be copied and employed until the second century of the Christian era.

It would appear that each chapter of the Book of the Dead had an independent origin, and it is probable that their inclusion and adoption into the body of the work were spread over many centuries, It is possible that some of the texts reflect changes in theological opinion, but each chapter stands by itself. It would seem, however, that there was a traditional order in the sequence of the chapters.

THE THREE RECENSIONS

There were three recensions or versions of the Book of the Dead - the Heliopolitan, the Theban, and the Saite. The Heliopolitan Recension was edited by the priests of the College of Anu, Or On, known to the Greeks as Heliopolis, and was based upon texts not now recoverable. The Pyramids of Unas, Teta, and Pepi contain the original texts of this recension, which represent the theological system introduced by the priests of Ra. The essentials of the primitive Egyptian religion are, however, retained, the only modification in them being the introduction of the solar doctrine of Ra. In later times the priesthood of Ra were forced to acknowledge the supremacy of Osiris, and this theological defeat is visible in the more modern texts. Between the sixth and eleventh dynasties the priests of On edited a number of fresh chapters from time to time.

The Thebas Recension was much in vogue from the eighteenth to the twenty-second dynasties, and was usually written upon papyri and painted upon coffins in hieroglyphs. Each chapter was preserved distinct from the others, but appears to have had no distinct place in the entire collection.

The Saite Recension was definitely arranged at some date prior to the twenty-sixth dynasty, and is written upon coffins and papyri, and also in hieratic and demotic script. It continued to be employed to the end of the Ptolemaic period.

As we have previously noticed, the Book of the Dead was for their use from the moment when they found themselves inhabitants of the other world. Magic was the very mainspring of existence in that sphere, and unless a spirit was acquainted with the formulæ which compelled the respect of the various gods and demons, and even of inanimate objects, it was helpless. The region to which the dead departed, the primitive Egyptians called Duat. They believed it to be formed of the body of Osiris. It was regarded as dark and gloomy, containing pits of fire and dreadful monsters which circled the earth, and was in its turn, bounded by a river and a lofty chain of mountains. The part of it that was nearest to Egypt was regarded as a description of mingled desert and forest, through which the soul of the deceased might not hope to struggle unless guided by some benevolent spirit who knew the paths through this country of despair. Thick darkness covered everything, and under the veil of this, the hideous inhabitants of the place practised all sorts of hostility to the newcomer, unless by the use of words of power he could prove his superiority over them. But there was one delectable part in this horrid region - the Sekhet Hetepet, the Elysian fields which contained the Sekhet Aaru, or the Field of Reeds, where dwelt the god Osiris and his company. At first he had domain over this part of the Duat alone, but gradually he succeeded in extending it over the entire country of the dead, of which he was monarch. We find also a god of the Duat named Duati, but who appears to have been more a personification of the region than anything else. Now the wish of all good men was to win to the kingdom of Osiris, and to that end they made an exhaustive study of the prayers and ritual of the Book of the Dead, in order that they might the more easily penetrate to the region of bliss. This they might reach by two ways - by land and by water. The path by water was no whit less dreadful than that by land, the passage of the soul being barred by streams of fire and boiling water, and the banks of the rivers navigated were populous with evil spirits.

SELECTIONS FROM THE "BOOK OF THE DEAD"

A HYMN TO THE SETTING SUN

A hymn of praise to Ra when he riseth upon the horizon, and when he getteth in the land of life. Osiris, the scribe Ani saith:

"Homage to thee, O Ra, when thou risest - as - Tem-Heru-khuti - Tem-Harmachis - Thou art adored - by me when-thy beauties are before mine eyes, and - when thy - radiance - falleth - upon - my - body. Thou goest forth to thy setting in the Sektet boat with - fair - winds, and thy heart is glad; the heart of the Mater boat rejoiceith. Thou stridest over the heavens in peace, and all thy foes are cast down; the never-resting stars sing hymns of praise unto thee, and the stars which rest, and the stars which never fail glorify thee as thou sinkest to rest in the horizon of Manu, O thou who art beautiful at morn and at eve, O thou lord who livest and art established, O my lord!

"Homage to thee, O thou who art Ra when thou risest, and. Tem when thou settest - in - beauty. Thou risest and shinest on the back of thy mother - Nut, - O thou who art crowned king of the gods! Nut doeth homage unto thee, and everlasting and never-changing order embraceth thee at morn and at eve. Thou stridest over the heaven, being glad of heart, and the Lake of Testes is content - thereat - . The Sebau Fiend hath fallen to the ground; his arms and his hands have been hacked off, and the knife hath severed the joints of his body. Ra hath a fair wind; the Sektet boat goeth forth and sailing along it cometh into port. The gods of the south and of the north, of the west and of the east, praise thee, O thou divine substance, from whom all forms of life come into being. Thou sendest forth the word, and the earth is flooded with silence, O thou only One, who didst dwell in heaven before ever the earth and the mountains came into existence. O runner, O Lord, O only One, thou maker of things which are, thou hast fashioned the tongue of the company of the gods, thou hast produced whatsoever cometh forth from the waters, and thou springest up from them over the flooded land of the Lake of Horus. Let me snuff the air which cometh forth from thy nostrils, and the nostrils, and the north wind which cometh forth from thy mother - Nut - . O, make thou to be glorious my shining form - khu - , O Osiris, make thou to be divine my soul - ba - ! Thou art worshipped - in - peace—or (in setting - , O Lord of the gods, thou are exalted by reason of thy wondrous works. Shine thou with the rays of light upon my body day by day, - upon me - , Osiris the scribe, the teller of the divine offerings of all the gods, the overseer of the granary of the lords of Abtu-Abydos - , the royal scribe in truth who loveth thee; Ani, victorious in peace."

HYMN AND LITANY TO OSIRIS

(From the Papyrus of Ani, British Museum, No. 10,470, sheet 19)

"Praise unto thee, O Osiris, lord of eternity, Unnefer, Heru-khuti - Harmachis - , whose forms are manifold, and whose attributes are majestic, Ptah-Seker-Tern in Annu - Heliopolis - , the lord of the hidden place, and the creator of Het-ka-Ptah - Memphis - and of the gods - therein - , the guide of the underworld, who, - the gods - glorify when thou settest in Nut. Isis embraceth thee in peace, and she driveth away the fiends from the mouth of thy path. Thou turnest thy face upon Amentet, and thou makest the earth to shine as with refined copper. Those who have lain down, i.e., the dead - rise up to see thee, they breathe the air and they look upon thy face when the Disk riseth on its horizon; their hearts are at peace inasmuch as they behold thee, O thou who art Eternity and Everlastingness!"

OPENING THE MOUTH OF OSIRIS

In one of the tombs of the New Stone Age was found a flint instrument which, as we know from inscriptions of the dynastic period, was used in performing the ceremony of "opening the mouth" of the dead, a fact that proves that even in the Old Stone Age a ceremony was performed on the dead body with the purpose of assisting the soul, or spirit, to acquire the faculties and powers needed by it in the other world. In this ceremony the flint instrument was thrust between the teeth of the dead man, and when these were separated his spirit form was believed. to acquire the power to eat and drink, to speak, to think, and to perform all the natural functions of the body.

The Chapter Of Opening The Mouth Of Osiris. The scribe Ani, triumphant, saith:

"May the good Ptah open my mouth, and may the god of my city loose the swathings, even the swathings which are over my mouth. Moreover, may Thoth, being filled and furnished with charms, come And loose the bandages, even the bandages of Set which fetter my mouth; and may the god Tem hurl them at those who would fetter - me - with them, and drive them back. May my mouth be opened, may my mouth be unclosed by Shu with his iron knife wherewith he opened the mouths of the gods. I am the goddess Sekhet, and I sit upon - my - place in the great wind (?) of heaven. I am the great goddess Sah who dwelleth among the Souls of Annu - Heliopolis - . Now as concerning every charm and all the words which may be spoken against me, may the gods resist them, and may each and every one of the company of the gods withstand them."

SOUL AND BODY
(From the Papyrus of Ani, British Museum, No. 10,470, sheet 17)
The chapter of Causing the Soul to be United to its Body in the Underworld. The Osiris Ani, triumphant, saith:

"Hail, thou god Anniu - i.e., Bringer! - Hail, thou god Pehrer - i.e., Runner - , who dwellest in thy hall! - Hail - , great God! Grant thou that my soul may come unto me from wheresoever it may be. If - it - would tarry, let then my soul be brought unto me from wherever it may be, for thou shalt find the Eye of Horns standing by thee like unto those beings who are like unto Osiris, and who

never lie down in death. Let not the Osiris Ani, triumphant, lie down in death among those who lie down in Annu, the land wherein souls are joined unto their bodies even in thousands. Let me have possession of my ba - soul - , and of my khu, and let me triumph therewith in every place wheresoever it may be. - Observe these things which - I - speak, for it hath staves with it; - observe then, O ye divine guardians of heaven, my soul-wheresoever it may be. - If it would tarry, do thou make my soul to look upon my body, for thou shalt find the Eye of Horus standing by thee like those - beings who are like unto Osiris - .

"Hail, ye gods, who tow along the boat of the lord of millions of years, who bring - it - above the underworld and who make it to travel over Nut, who make souls to enter into - their - spiritual bodies, whose hands are filled with your ropes and who clutch your weapons tight, destroy ye the Enemy; thus shall the boat of the sun be glad and the great God shall set out on his journey in peace. And behold, grant ye that the soul of Osiris Ani, triumphant, may come forth before the gods and that it may be triumphant along with you in the eastern part of the sky to follow unto the place where it was yesterday; - and that it may have - peace, peace in Amentet. May it look upon its material body, may it rest upon its spiritual body; and may its body neither perish nor suffer corruption forever."

(These words are to be said over a soul of gold inlaid with precious stones and placed on the breast of Osiris.)

OF EVIL RECOLLECTIONS

(From the Papyrus of Nu, British Museum, No. 10,477, sheet 8)

The chapter of driving evil recollections from the mouth. The overseer of the palace, the chancellor-in-chief, Nu, triumphant, the son of the overseer of the palace, the chancellor-in-chief, Amen-hetep, triumphant, saith:

"Hail, thou that cuttest off heads, and slitteth brows, thou being who puttest away the memory of evil things from the mouth of the Khus by means of the incantations which they have within them, look not upon me with the - same - eyes with which thou lookest upon them. Go thou round about on thy legs, and let thy face be - turned - behind thee so that thou mayest be able to see the divine slaughterers of the god Shu who are coming up behind thee to cut off thy head, and to slit thy brow by reason of the message of violence - sent - by thy lord, and to see (?) that which thou sayest. Work thou for me so that the memory of evil things shall dart from my mouth; let not my head be cut off; let not my brow be slit; and let not my mouth be shut fast by reason of the incantations which thou hast within thee, according to that which thou doest for the Khus through the incantations which they have within themselves. Get thee back and depart at the - sound of - the two speeches which the goddess Isis uttered when thou didst come to cast the recollection of evil things unto the. mouth of Osiris by the will of Suti his enemy, saying, 'Let thy face be toward the privy parts, and look upon that face which cometh forth from the flame of the Eye of Horus against thee from within the Eye of Tem,' and the calamity of that night which shall consume thee. And Osiris went back, for the abomination of thee was in him; and thou didst go back, for the abomination of him is in thee. I have gone back, for the abomination of thee is in me; and thou shalt go back, for the abomination of me is in thee. Thou wouldst come unto me, but I say that thou shalt not advance to me so that I come to an end, and - I - say then to the divine slaughterers of the god Shu, 'Depart.'"

OF RESCUE

(From the Papyrus of Nu, British Museum, No. 10,477, sheet 6)

The chapter of not letting the soul of Nu, triumphant, be captive in the underworld. He saith:

"Hail, thou who art exalted! - Hail - thou who art adored! O thou mighty one of Souls, thou divine Soul, thou possessor of terrible power, who dost put the fear of thyself into the gods, thou who art crowned upon thy throne of majesty, I pray thee to make a way for the ba - soul - , and for the khu, and the khaibit - shade - of the overseer of the palace, the chancellor-in-chief, Nu, triumphant - and let him be - provided therewith. I am a perfect khu, and I have made - my - way unto the place wherein dwell Ra and Hathor."

(If this chapter be known - by the deceased - he shall be able to transform himself into a khu provided - with his soul and with his shade - in the underworld, and he shall never be held captive at any door in Amentet, in entering in or in coming out.)

OF OPENING THE TOMB

(From the Papyrus of Nebseni, British Museum, No. 9,900, sheet 6)

The chapter of opening the tomb of the soul - and - to the shade of Osiris the scribe Nebseni, the lord of reverence, born of the lady of the house, Mut-restha, triumphant, so that he may come forth by day and have dominion over his fleet. He saith:

"That which was shut fast hath been opened, that is to say, he that lay down in death - hath been opened - . That which was open hath been shut to my soul through the command of the Eye of Horus, which hath strengthened me and which maketh to stand fast the beauties which are upon the forehead of Ra, whose strides are long as - he - lifteth up - his - legs - in journeying - . I have made for myself a way, my members are mighty and are strong. I am Horus the avenger of his divine father. I am he who bringeth along his divine father, and who bringeth along his mother by means of his sceptre (?), And the way shall be opened unto him who hath gotten dominion over his feet, and he shall see the Great God in the Boat of Ra, - when - souls are counted therein at the bows, and when the years are also counted up. Grant that the eye of Horus, which maketh the adornments of light to be firm upon the forehead of Ra, may deliver my soul for me, and let there be darkness upon your faces, O ye who would hold fast Osiris. Oh, keep not captive my soul, Oh, keep not ward over my shade, but let a way be opened for my soul - and - and for my shade, and let - them - see the Great God in the shrine on the day of the judgment of souls, and let - them - recite the utterances of Osiris, whose habitations are hidden, to those who guard the members of Osiris, and who keep ward over the Khus, and who hold captive the shades of the dead who would work evil against me, so that they shall - not - work evil against me. May a way for thy double - Ka - along with thee and along with - thy - soul be prepared by those who keep ward over the members of Osiris, and who bold captive the shades of the dead. Heaven shall - not - keep thee, the earth shall - not - hold thee captive, thou shalt not have they being with the divine beings who make slaughter, but thou shalt have dominion over thy legs, and thou shalt advance to thy body straightway in the earth - and to - those who belong to the shrine and guard the members of Osiris."

OF NOT SAILING TO THE EAST

(From the Papyrus of Nu, British Museum, No. 10,477, sheet 6)

The chapter of not sailing to the east in the underworld. The chancellor-in-chief, Nu, triumphant, saith:

"Hail, phallus of Ra, who departest from thy calamity - which ariseth - through opposition (?), the cycles have been without movement for millions of years. I am stronger than the strong, I am mightier than the mighty. If I sail away or if I be snatched away to the east through the two horns," or - as others say -

"if any evil and abominable thing be done unto me at the feast of the devils, the phallus of Ra shall be swallowed up, - along with - the head of Osiris. And behold me, for I journey along over the fields wherein the gods mow down those who make reply unto - their words - ; now verily the two horns of the god Khepera shall be thrust aside, and verily pus shall spring into being in the eye of Tem along with corruption if I be kept in restraint, or if I have gone toward the east, or if the feast of devils be made in my presence, or if any malignant wound be inflicted upon me."

OF BEING NIGH UNTO THOTH

(From the Papyrus of Nu, British Museum, No. 10,477, sheet 7)

The chapter of being nigh unto Thoth. The chancellor-in-chief, Nu, triumphant, saith:

"I am he who sendeth forth terror into the powers of rain and thunder, and I ward off from the great divine lady the attacks of violence - I have smitten like the god Shat - i.e., the god of slaughter - , and I have out libations of cool water like the god Ashu, and I have worked for the great divine lady - to ward off - the attacks of violence - , I have made to flourish - my - knife along with the knife which is in the hand of Thoth in the powers of rain and thunder."

OF BEING NIGH UNTO THOTH

(From the Papyrus of Nu, British Museum, No. 10,477, sheets 19 and 20)

The chapter of being nigh unto Thoth and of giving glory unto a man in the underworld. The chancellor-in-chief, Nu, triumphant, saith:

"I am the god Her-ab-maat - i.e., 'he that is within his eye - , and I have come to give right and truth to Ra; I have made Suti to be at peace with me by means of offerings made to the god Aker, and to the Tesgeru deities, and by - making - reverence unto Seb."

The following - words are to be recited in the Sektet boat: " - Hail, - sceptre of Anubis, I have made the four Khus who are in the train of the lord of the universe to be at peace with me, and I am the lord of the fields through their decree. I am the divine father Bah - i.e., the god of the water flood - , and I do away with the thirst of him that keepeth ward over the Lakes. Behold ye me, then, O great gods of majesty who dwell among the Souls of Annu, for I am lifted up over you. I am the god Menkh - i.e., Gracious One - who dwelleth among you. Verily I have cleansed my soul, O great god of majesty, set not before me the evil obstacles which issue from thy mouth, and let not destruction come round about me, or upon me. I have made myself clean in the Lake of making to be at peace, - and in the Lake of - weighing in the balance, and I have bathed myself in Netert-utchat, which is under the holy sycamore tree of heaven. Behold - I am - bathed, - and I have - triumphed - over - all - mine enemies - straightway who come forth and rise up against right and truth. I am right and true in earth. I, even I, have spoken (?)

with my mouth - which is - the power of the Lord, the Only one, Ra the mighty, who liveth upon right and truth. Let not injury be inflicted upon me, - but let me be - clothed on the day of those who go forward (?) to every - good - thing."

OF BRINGING A BOAT ALONG IN HEAVEN

(From the Papyrus of Nu, British Museum, No. 10,477, sheet 9)

The chapter of bringing along a boat in heaven. The chancellor-in-chief, triumphant, saith:

"Hail to thee, O thou Thigh which dwelleth in the northern heaven in the Great Lake, which art seen and which dieth not. I have stood up over thee when thou didst rise like a god. I have seen thee, and I have not lain down in death; I have stood over thee, and I have risen like a god. I have cackled like a goose, and I have alighted like a hawk by the divine clouds and by the great dew. I have journeyed from the earth to heaven. The god Shu - made - me to stand up, the god of Light hath made me to be vigorous by the two sides of the ladder, and the stars which never rest set - me - on - my - way and bring - me - away from slaughter. I bring along with me the things which drive back calamities as I advance over the passage of the god Pen; thou comest, how great art thou, O god Pen! I have come from the Pool of Flame which is in the Sekhet-Sasa - i.e., the Field of Fire. - Thou livest in the Pool of Flame in Sekhet-Sasa, and I live upon the staff of the hold - god. Hail, thou god Kaa, who dost bring those things which are in the boats by the . . . I stand up in the boat and I guide myself - over - the water: I have stood up in the boat and the god hath guided me. I have stood up. I have spoken. - I am master of the - crops. I sail round about as I go forward, and the gates which are in Sekhem - Letopolis - are opened unto me, and fields are awarded unto me in the city of Unni - Hermopolis - , and laborers (?) are given unto me together with those of my own flesh and bone."

OF PROTECTING THE BOAT OF RA

(From the Papyrus of Nu, British Museum, No. 10,477, sheet 97)

The chapter of protecting the boat of Ra. "O thou that cleavest the water as thou comest forth from the stream and dost sit upon thy place in thy boat, sit thou upon thy place in thy boat as thou goest forth to thy station of yesterday, and do thou join the Osiris, the overseer of the palace, the chancellor-in-chief, Nu, triumphant, the perfect Khu, unto thy mariners, and let thy strength be his strength.

"Hail, Ra, in thy name of Ra, if thou dost pass by the eye of seven cubits, which hath a pupil of three cubits, then verily do thou strengthen the Osiris, Nu, triumphant, the perfect Khu, - let him be among - thy mariners, and let thy strength be his strength. Hail, Ra, in thy name of Ra, if thou dost pass by those who are overturned in death, then verily do thou make the Osiris, Nu, triumphant, the perfect soul, to stand up upon his feet, and may thy strength be his strength.

Hail, Ra, in thy name of Ra, if the hidden things of the underworld are opened unto thee and thou dost gratify (?) the heart of the cycle of thy gods, then verily do thou grant joy of heart unto the. chancellor-in-chief, Nu, triumphant, and let thy strength be his strength. Thy members, O Ra, are established by - this - Chapter (?)."

- This Chapter - shall be recited over a bandlet of the fine linen of kings - upon which - it hath been written with Anti, which shall be laid upon the neck of the perfect Khu on the way of the burial. If this amulet be laid upon his neck he shall do everything which he desireth to do even like the gods; and he shall join himself unto the followers of Horus; and he shall be established as a star face to face with Septet - Sothis - ; and his corruptible body shall be as a god along with his kinsfolk forever; and the goddess Menqet shall make plants to germinate upon his body; and the Majesty of the God Thoth lovingly shall make the light to rest upon his corruptible body at will, even as he did for the majesty of the King of the North and of the South, the god Osiris, triumphant.

ON GOING INTO THE BOAT OF RA

(From the Papyrus of Nu, British Museum, No. 10,177, sheet 28)

The chapter of going into the boat of Ra. The chancellor-in-chief, Nu, triumphant, saith:

"Hail, thou Great God who art in thy boat, bring thou me into thy boat. - I have come forward to thy steps - , let me be the director of thy journeyings and let me be among those who belong to thee and who are among the stars which never rest. The things which are an abomination unto thee and the things which are an abomination unto me I will not eat, that which is an abomination unto me, that which is an abomination unto me is filth and I will not eat thereof; but sepulchral offerings and holy food - will I eat - , and I shall not be overthrown thereby. I will not draw nigh unto filth with my hands, and I will not walk thereon with my sandals, because my bread - is made - of white barley, and my ale - is made - of red barley; and behold, the Sektet boat and the Atet boat have brought these things and have laid the gifts (?) of the lands upon the altar of the Souls of Annu. Hymns of praise be to thee. O Ur-arit-s, as thou travellest through heaven! Let there be food - for thee - , O dweller in the city of Teni - this - , and when the dogs gather together let me not suffer harm. I myself have come, and I have delivered the god from the things which have been inflicted upon him, and from the grievous sickness of the body of the arm, and of the leg. I have come and I have spit upon the body, I have bound up the arm, and I have made the leg to walk. - I have - entered - the boat - and - I - sail round about by the command of Ra."

OF KNOWING THE SOULS OF THE EAST

(From the Papyrus of Nu, British Museum, No. 10,477, sheet 19)

The chapter of knowing the souls of the east. The chancellor-in-chief, Nu, triumphant, saith:

"I, even I, know the eastern gate of heaven - now its southern part is at the Lake of Kharu and its northern part is at the canal of the geese - whereout Ra cometh with the winds which make him to advance. I am he who is concerned with the tackle (?) - which is - in the divine bark, I am the sailor who ceaseth not on the boat of Ra. I, even I, know the two sycamores of turquoise between which Ra showed himself when he strideth forward over the supports of Shu[36] toward the gate of the lord of the East through which Ra cometh forth. I, even I, know the Sekhet-Aarru of Ra, the walls of which are of iron. The height of the wheat therein is five cubits, of the cars thereof two cubits, and the stalks thereof three cubits. The barley therein is - in height - seven cubits, the ears thereof are three cubits, and the stalks thereof are four cubits. And behold, the Khus, each one of whom therein is nine cubits in height, reap is near the divine Souls of the East. I, even I, know the divine Souls of the East, that is to say, Heru-khuti - Harmachis - , and the Calf of the goddess Khera, and the Morning Star - daily. A divine city hath been built for me, I know it, and I know the name thereof; 'Sekhet-Aarru' is its name."

OF SEKHET-HETEPET

(From the Papyrus, of Nebseni, British Museum, No. 9,900, sheet 17)

Here begin the chapters of Sekhet-Hetepet, and the chapters Of Coming Forth By Day; of going into and of coming out from the underworld; of coming to Sekhet-Aaru; of being in Sekhet, the mighty land, the lady of winds; of having power there; of becoming a Khu there; of ploughing there; of eating there; of drinking there; of making love there; and of doing everything even as a man doeth upon earth. Behold the scribe and artist of the Temple of Ptah, Nebseni, who saith:

"Set hath taken possession of Horus, who looked with the two eyes upon the building (?) round Sekhet-Hetepet, but I have unfettered Horus - and taken him from - Set, and Set hath opened the ways of the two eyes - which are - in heaven. Set hath cast (?) his moisture to the winds upon the soul - that hath - his day - or his eye - and who dwelleth in the city of Mert, and he hath delivered the interior of the body of Horus from the gods of Akert. Behold me now, for I make this mighty boat to travel over the Lake of Hetep, and I brought it away with might from the palace of Shu; the domain of his stars groweth young and reneweth its former strength. I have brought the boat into the lakes thereof so that I may come forth into the cities thereof, and I have sailed into their divine city Hetep. And behold, it is because I, even I, am at Peace with his seasons, and with his guidance, and with his territory, and with the company of gods who are his first born. He maketh the two divine fighters—(i.e., Horus and Set) - to be at peace with those who watch over the living ones whom he hath created in fair form, and he bringeth peace - with him - ; he maketh the two divine fighters to be at peace with those who watch over them. He cutteth off the hair from the divine fighters, be driveth away storm from the helpless, and he keepeth harm from the Khus. Let me gain dominion within that Field, for I know it, and I have sailed among its lakes so that I might come into the cities. My mouth is strong; and I am equipped - with weapons to use - against the Khus; let them not have dominion over me. Let me be rewarded with thy fields, O thou a god Hetep; that which is thy wish, shalt thou do, O lord of the winds. May I become a khu therein, may I eat therein, may I drink therein, may I plough therein, may I reap therein, may I fight therein, may I make love therein, may my words be mighty therein, may I never be in a state of servitude therein, but may I be in authority therein. Thou hast made strong (?) the mouth and the throat (?) of the god Hetep; Qetetbu is its (?) name. He is established upon the watery supports (?) of the god Shu, and is linked unto the pleasant things of Ra. He is the divider of years, he is hidden of mouth, his mouth is silent, that which he uttereth is secret, he fulfilleth eternity and taketh possession of everlastingness of existence as Hetep, the lord Hetep. The god Horus maketh himself to be strong like unto the Hawk which is one thousand cubits in length and two thousand - cubits in width - in life; he hath equipments with him, and he journeyeth on and cometh where the seat of his heart wisheth in the Pools thereof and in the cities thereof. He was begotten in the birth-chamber of the god of the city, he hath offerings - made unto him - of the food of the god of the city, he performeth that which is meet to do therein, and the union thereof, in the matter of everything of the birth-chamber of the divine city. When - he - setteth in life like crystal he performeth everything therein, and these things are like unto the things which are done in the Lake of double Fire, wherein there is none that rejoiceth, and wherein are all manner of evil things. The god Hetep goeth in, and cometh out, and goeth backward - in - that, Field that gathereth together all manner of things for the birth-chamber of the god of the city. When he setteth in life like crystal he performeth all manner of things therein which are like unto the things which are done in the Lake of double Fire, wherein there is none that rejoiceth, and wherein are no evil things whatsoever. - Let me - live with the god Hetep, clothed and not despoiled by the lords of the north (?) and may the lords of divine things bring food unto me; may he make me to go forward and may I come forth, and may he bring my power to me there, and may I receive it, and may my equipment be from the god Hetep. May I gain the mastery over the great and mighty word which is in my body in this my place, and by it I will remember and I will forget. Let me go forward in my journey, and let me plough. I am at peace in the divine city[37], and I know the waters, cities, nomes, and lakes which are in Sekhet-hetep. I exist therein, I am strong therein, I become a khu therein, I eat therein, I sow seed therein, I reap the harvest therein, I plough therein, I make love therein, I am at peace with the god Hetep therein. Behold I scatter seed therein, I sail about among its lakes and I come forward to the cities thereof, O divine Hetep. Behold my mouth is equipped with thy horns

- for teeth - , grant me an overflowing supply of the food whereon the kas and khus - live - . I have passed the judgment of Shu upon him that knoweth him, so that I may go forth to the cities thereof, and may sail about among its lakes and may walk about in Sekhet-hetep; and behold, Ra is in heaven, and behold, the god Hetep is its double offering. I have come onward to its land, I have put on my girdle (?), I have come forth so that the gifts which are about to be given unto me may be given, I have made gladness for myself. I have laid hold upon my strength which the god Hetep hath greatly increased for me. O Unen-em-hetep,[38] I have entered into thee and my soul followeth after me, and my divine food is upon both my hands, O Lady of the two lands,[39] who establishest my word whereby I remember and forget; I would live without injury, without any injury - being done - unto me, oh, grant to me, oh, do thou grant to me, joy of heart. Make thou me to be at peace, bind thou up my sinews and muscles, and make me to receive the air. O Un (en)-em-hetep, thou Lady of the winds, I have entered into thee and I have opened - i.e., shown - my head. Ra falleth asleep, but I am awake, and there is the goddess Hast at the gate of heaven by night. Obstacles have been set before me, but I have gathered together what he hath emitted. I am in my city. O Nut-urt,[40] I have entered into thee and I have counted my harvest, and I go forward to Uakh.[41] I am the bull enveloped in turquoise, the lord of the Field of the Bull, the lord of the divine speech of the goddess Septer - Sothis - at her hours. O Uakh, I have entered into thee, I have eaten my bread, I have gotten the mastery over choice pieces of the flesh of oxen and of feathered fowl, and the birds of Shu have been given unto me; I follow after the gods and - I come after - the divine kas. O Tchefet,[42] I have entered in to thee. I array myself in apparel, and I gird myself with the sa garment of Ra; now behold, - he is - in heaven and those who dwell therein follow Ra, and - I - follow Ra in heaven. O Unen-em-hetep, lord of the two lands, I have entered into thee, and I have plunged into the lakes of Tchesert; behold me, for all filth hath departed from me. The Great God groweth therein, and behold, I have found - food therein - ; I have snared feathered fowl and I feed upon the finest - of them - . O Qenqentet,[43] I have entered into thee, and I have seen the Osiris - my father - , and I have gazed upon my mother, and I have made love. I have caught the worms and serpents, and I am delivered. And I know the name of the god who is opposite to the goddess Tchesert, and who hath straight hair and is equipped with two horns; he reapeth, and I both plough and reap. O Hast, I have entered in to thee, I have driven back those who would come to the turquoise - sky - , and I have followed the winds of the company of the gods. The Great God hath given my head unto me, and he who hath bound on me my head is the Mighty one who hath turquoise (?) eyes, namely, Ari-en-ab-f - i.e., he doeth as he pleaseth - . O Usert,[44] I have come into thee at the head of the house wherein divine food is brought for me. O Smam,[45] I have come into thee. My heart watcheth, my head is equipped with the white crown, I am led into celestial regions, and I make to flourish terrestrial objects, and there is joy of heart for the Bull, and for celestial beings, and for the company of the gods. I am the god who is the Bull, the lord of the gods, as he goeth forth from the turquoise - sky - -. O divine nome of wheat and barley, I have come into thee, I have come forward to thee and I have taken up that which followeth me, namely the best of the libations of the company of the gods. I have tied up my boat in the celestial lakes, I have lifted up the post at which to anchor, I have recited the prescribed words with my voice, and I have ascribed praise unto the gods who dwell in Sekhet-hetep."

OF KNOWING THE SOULS OF PE

(From the Papyrus of Nu, British Museum, No. 10,477, sheet 18)

Another chapter of knowing the souls of Pe. The overseer of the palace, the chancellor-in-chief, Nu, triumphant, saith:

" - Hail, - Khat, who dwellest in Khat, in Anpet,[46] and in the nome of Khat! - Hail, - ye goddesses of the class who dwell in the city of Pe, ye celestial lands (?), ye stars, and ye divine beings, who give cakes and ale (?), do ye know for what reason the city of Pe hath been given unto Horus? I, even I, know though ye knoweth it not. Behold Ra gave the city unto him in return for the injury in his eye, for which cause Ra said to Horus, 'Let me see what is coming to pass in thine eye,' and forthwith he looked thereat. Then Ra said to Horus, 'Look at that black pig,' and he looked, and straightway an injury was done unto his eye, - namely - , a mighty storm - took place - . Then said Horus unto Ra, 'Verily, my eye seems as if it were an eye upon which Suti had inflicted a blow'; - and thus saying - he ate his heart.[47] Then said Ra to those gods, 'Place ye him in his chamber, and he shall do well.' Now the black pig was Suti who had transformed himself into a black pig, and it was he who had aimed the blow of fire which was in the eye of Horus. Then said Ra unto those gods, 'The pig is an abominable thing unto Horus; oh, but he shall do well although the pig is an abomination unto him.' Then the company of the gods, who were among the divine followers of Horus when he existed in the form of his own child, said, 'Let sacrifice be made - to the gods - of his bulls, and of his goats, and of his pigs.' Now the father of Mesthi, Hapi, Tuamautef and Qebhsennuf is Horus, and their mother is Isis. Then said Horus to Ra, 'Give me two divine brethren in the city of Pe and two divine brethren in the city of Nekhen, who - have sprung - from my body and who shall be with me in the guise of everlasting judges, then shall the earth blossom and thunderclouds and rain be blotted out.' And the name of Horus became 'Her-uatch-f' - i.e., Prince of his emerald stone. - I, even I, know the Souls of Pe, namely, Horus, Mesthi, and Hapi."

OF THE SWALLOW

(From the Papyrus of Nu, British Museum, No. 10,477, sheet 10)

The chapter of making the transformation into a swallow. The chancellor-in-chief, Nu, triumphant, saith:

"I am a swallow, I am a swallow. I am the scorpion, the daughter of Ra. Hail, ye gods, whose scent is sweet; hail, ye gods, whose scent is sweet I - Hail - , Flame, which cometh forth from the horizon! Hail, thou who art in the city, I have brought the Warden of his Bight therein. Oh, stretch out unto me thy hand so that I may be able to pass my days in the Pool of Double Fire, and let me advance with my message, for I have come with words to tell. Oh, open - thou - the doors to me and I will declare the things which have been seen by me. Horus hath become the divine Prince of the Boat of the Sun, and unto him hath been given the throne of his divine father Osiris, and Set, that son of Nut, - lieth - under the fetters which he had made for me. I have made a computation of what is in the city of Sekhem, I have stretched out both my hands and arms at the word (?) of Osiris, I have passed on to judgment, and I have come that - I - may speak, grant that I may pass on and declare my tidings. I enter in, - I - am-judged, and - I - come forth worthy at the gate of Neb-er-tcher. I am pure at the great place of the passage of souls, I have done away with my sins, I have put away mine offences, and I have destroyed the evil which appertained unto my members upon earth. Hail, ye divine beings who guard the doors, make ye for me a way, for, behold, I am like unto you. I have come forth by day, I have journeyed on, on my legs, and I have gained the mastery over my footsteps - before - the God of Light, I know the hidden ways and the doors of the Sekhet-Aaru, verily I, even I, have come. I have overthrown mine enemies upon earth, and yet my perishable body is in the gravel"

If this chapter be known - by the deceased - he shall come forth by day, he shall not be turned back at any gate in the underworld, and he shall make his transformation into a swallow regularly and continually.

TRANSFORMATION INTO A LOTUS

(From the Papyrus of Nu, British Museum, No. 10,477, sheet 11)

The chapter of making the transformation into a lotus. The overseer of the palace, the chancellor-in-chief, Nu, saith:

"I am the pure Lotus which springeth up from the divine splendor that belongeth to the nostrils of Ra. I have made - my way - , and I follow on seeking for him who is Horus. I am the pure one who cometh forth out of the Field."

TRANSFORMATION INTO A LOTUS

(From the Papyrus of Paqrer - see Naville, op. cit., Bd. I, Bl. 93)

The chapter of making the transformation into a lotus. Saith Osiris Paqrer:

"Hail, thou lotus, thou type of the god Nefer-Temu! I am the man that knoweth you, and I know your names among - those of - the gods, the lords of the underworld, and I am one of you. Grant ye that - I - may see the gods who are the divine guides in the Tuat - underworld, - and grant ye unto me a place in the underworld near unto the lords of Amentet. Let me arrive at a habitation in the land of Tchesert, and receive me, O all ye gods, in the presence of the lords of eternity. Grant that my soul may come forth whithersoever it pleaseth, and let it not be driven away from the presence of the great company of Gods."

TRANSFORMATION INTO PTAH
(From the Papyrus of Nu, British Museum, No. 10,477, sheets 9 and 10)
The chapter of making the transformation into Ptah, of eating cakes, and of drinking ale, and of unfettering the steps, and of becoming a living being in Annu - Heliopolis. The chancellor-in-chief, Nu, triumphant, saith:
"I fly like a hawk, I cackle like the smen goose, and I preach upon that abode of the underworld - aat - on the festival of the great Being. That which is an abomination unto me, I have not eaten; filth is an abomination unto me and I have not eaten thereof, and that which is an abomination unto my ka hath not entered into my belly. Let me, then, live upon that which the gods and the Khus decree for me; let me live and let me have power over cakes; let me eat them before the gods and the Khus - who have a favor - unto me; let me have power over - these cakes - and let me eat of them under the - shade of the - leaves of the palm tree of the goddess Hathor, who is my divine Lady. Let the offering of the sacrifice, and the offering of cakes, and vessels of libations be made in Annu; let me clothe myself in the taau garment - which I shall receive - from the hand of the goddess Tait; let me stand up and let me sit down wheresoever I please. My head is like unto that of Ra, and - when my members are - gathered together - I am - like unto Tem; the four - sides of the domain - of Ra, and the width of the earth four times. I come forth. My tongue is like unto that of Ptah and my throne is like unto that of the goddess Hathor, and I make mention of the words of Tem, my father, with my mouth. He it is who constraineth the handmaid, the wife of Seb, and before him are bowed - all - heads, and there is fear of him. Hymns of praise are repeated for - me - by reason of - my - mighty acts, and I am decreed to be the divine Heir of Seb, the lord of the earth, and to be the protector therein. The god Seb refresheth me, and he maketh his risings to be mine. Those who dwell in Annu bow down their heads unto me, for I am their lord and I am their bull. I am more powerful than the lord of time, and I shall enjoy the pleasures of love, and shall gain the mastery over millions of years.

OF PERFORMING TRANSFORMATIONS
(From the Papyrus of Nu, British Museum, No. 10,477, sheet 10)
The chapter of performing the transformation into a hawk of gold. The chancellor-in-chief, Nu, triumphant, saith:
"I have risen, I have risen like a mighty hawk - of gold - that cometh forth from his egg; I fly and I alight like the hawk which hath a back four cubits wide, and the wings of which are Eke unto the mother-of-emerald of the south. I have

come forth from the interior of the Sektet boat, and my heart hath been brought unto me from the mountain of the east. I have alighted upon the Atet boat, and those who were dwelling in their companies have been brought unto me, and they bowed low in paying homage unto me and in saluting me with cries of joy. I have risen, I have gathered myself together like the beautiful hawk of gold, which hath the head of a Bennu bird, and Ra entereth in day by day to hearken unto my words; I have taken my seat among those first-born gods of Nut. I am established, and the divine Sekhet-hetep is before me, I have eaten therein, I have become a khu therein, I have an abundance therein - as much as I desire - the god Nepra hath given to me my throat, and I have gained the mastery over that which guardeth - or belongeth to - my head."

COMING FORTH BY DAY

(From the Papyrus of Mes-em-neter, Naville, op. cit., Bd. I, Bl. 81)

Another chapter:

"I am the Fire-god, the divine brother of the Fire-god, and - I am - Osiris the brother of Isis. My divine son, together with his mother Isis, hath avenged me on mine enemies. My enemies have wrought every - kind of - evil, therefore their arms, and hands, and feet, have been fettered by reason of their wickedness which they have wrought upon me. I am Osiris, the first-born of the divine womb, the first-born of the gods, and the heir of my father Osiris-Seb (?). I am Osiris, the lord of the heads that live, mighty of breast and powerful of back, with a phallus which goeth to the remotest limits - where - -men and women - live - . I am Sah - Orion - who travelleth over his domain and who journeyeth along before the stars of heaven, - which is - the belly of my mother Nut; she conceived me through her love, and she gave birth to me because it was her will to do so. I am Anpu - Anubis—on the day of the god Sepa. I am the Bull at the head of the meadow. I, even I, am Osiris who imprisoned his father together with his mother on the day of making the great slaughter; now - his - father is Seb, and - his - mother is Nut. I am Horus, the first-born of Ra of the risings. I am Anpu - Anubis - on the day of - the god Sepa. I, even I, am the lord Tem. I am Osiris. Hail, thou divine first-born, who dost enter and dost speak before the divine Scribe and Doorkeeper of Osiris, grant that I may come. I have become a khu, I have been judged, I have become a divine being, I have come, and I have avenged mine own body. I have taken up my seat by the divine birth-chamber of Osiris, and I have destroyed the sickness and suffering which were there. I have become mighty, and I have become a divine being by the side of the birth-chamber of Osiris, I am brought forth with him, I renew my youth, I take possession of my two thighs which are in the place where is Osiris, and I open the mouth of the gods therewith, I take my seat by his side, and Thoth cometh forth, and - I am - strengthened in heart with thousands of cakes upon the altars of my divine father, and with my beasts, and with my cattle, and with my red feathered fowl, and with my oxen, and with my geese, and with my ducks, for Horus my Chieftain, and with the offerings which I make to Thoth, and with the sacrifices which I offer up to An-heri-ertaitsa."

THE CHAPTER OF BRINGING CHARMS TO OSIRIS

(From the Papyrus of Ani, British Museum, No. 10,470, sheet 15)

The chapter of bringing charms unto Osiris Ani - in the underworld. He saith:

"I am Tem-Khepera, who brought himself into being upon the thigh of his divine mother. Those who are in Nu - i.e., the sky - are made wolves, and those who are among the sovereign princes are become hyenas. Behold, I gather together the charm - from every place where - it is, and from every man with whom it is, swifter than greyhounds and quicker than light. Hail, thou who towest along the Makhent boat of Ra, the stays of thy sails and of thy rudder are taut in the wind as thou sailest up the Pool of Fire in the underworld. Behold, thou gatherest together the charm from every place where it is, and from every man with whom it is, swifter than greyhounds and quicker than light, - the charm - which created the forms of being from the . . . mother, and which either created the gods or maketh them silent, and which giveth the heat of fire unto the gods. Behold, the charm is given unto me, from wherever it is - and from him with whom it is - , swifter than greyhounds and quicker than light," or - as others say - "quicker than a shadow."

THE CHAPTER OF MEMORY

(From the Papyrus of Nu, British Museum, No. 10,477, sheet 5)

The chapter of making a man to possess memory in the underworld. The chancellor-in-chief, Nu, triumphant, the overseer of the palace, the son of the chief chancellor Amen-hetep, saith:

"May my name be given to me in the Great House, and may I remember my name in the House of Fire on the night of counting the years and of telling the number of the months. I am with the Divine One, and I sit on the eastern side of heaven. If any god whatsoever should advance unto me, let me be able to proclaim his name forthwith."

THE CHAPTER OF GIVING A HEART TO OSIRIS

(From the Papyrus of Ani, British Museum, No. 10,470, sheet 15)

The chapter of giving a heart to Osiris Ani in the underworld. He saith:

"May my heart - ah - be with me in the House of Hearts! May my heart - hat - be with me in the House of Hearts! May my heart be with me, and may it rest there, - or - I shall not eat of the cakes of Osiris on the eastern side of the Lake of Flowers, neither shall I have a boat wherein to go down the Nile, nor another wherein to go up, nor shall I be able to sail down the Nile with thee. May my mouth - be given - to me that I may speak therewith, and my two legs to walk therewith, and my two hands and arms to overthrow my foe. May the doors of heaven be opened unto me; may Seb, the Prince of the gods, open wide his two jaws unto me, may he open my two eyes which are blindfolded; may he cause me to stretch apart my two legs which are bound together; and may Anpu-Anubis - make my thighs firm so that I may stand upon them. May the goddess Sekhet make me to rise so that I may ascend unto heaven, and may that be done which I command in the House of ka - double - of Ptah - i.e., Memphis - . I understand with my heart. I have gained the mastery over my heart, I have gained the mastery over my two hands, I have gained the mastery over my legs, I have gained the power to do whatsoever my ka - double - pleaseth. My soul shall not be fettered to my body at the gates of the underworld; but I shall enter in peace and I shall come forth in peace."

LITANY

"Homage to thee, - O Lord of - starry deities in Annu, and of heavenly things in Kher-aba; thou god Unti, who art more glorious than the gods who are hidden in Annu; O grant thou unto me a path wherein I may pass in peace, for I am just and true; I have not spoken lies wittingly, nor have I done aught with deceit."

"Homage to thee, O An in Antes, (?) Heru-khuti - Harmachis - , with long strides thou stridest over heaven, O Heru-khuti. O grant thou unto me a path whereon I may pass in peace, for I am just and true; I have not spoken lies wittingly, nor have I done aught with deceit."

"Homage to thee, O Soul of everlastingness, thou Soul who dwellest in Tattu, Unnefer, son of Nut; thou art lord of Akert. O grant thou unto me a path whereon I may pass in peace, for I am just and true; I have not spoken lies wittingly, nor have I done aught with deceit."

"Homage to thee in thy dominion over Tattu; the Ureret crown is established upon thy head; thou art the One who maketh the strength which protecteth himself, and thou dwellest in peace in Tattu. O grant thou unto me a path whereon I may pass in peace, for I am just and true; I have not spoken lies wittingly, nor have I done aught with deceit."

"Homage to thee, O lord of the Acacia tree, the Seker boat is set upon its sledge; thou turnest back the Fiend, the worker of evil, and thou causest the Utchat to rest upon its seat. Oh, grant thou unto me a path whereon I may pass in peace, for I am just and true; I have not spoken lies wittingly, nor have I done aught with deceit."

"Homage to thee, O thou art mighty in thine hour, thou great and mighty Prince, dweller in An-rut-f,[48] lord of eternity and creator of everlastingness, thou art the lord of Suten-henen - Heracleopolis Magna - . Oh, grant thou unto me a path whereon I may pass in peace, for I am just and true; I have not spoken lies wittingly, nor have I done aught with deceit."

"Homage to thee, O thou who restest upon Right and Truth, thou art the lord of Abtu-Abydos - , and thy limbs are joined unto Tatches-ertet; thou art he to whom fraud and guile are hateful. Oh, grant thou unto me a path whereon I may pass in peace, for I am just and true; I have not spoken lies wittingly, nor have I done aught with deceit."

"Homage to thee, O thou who art within thy boat, thou bringest Hapi - i.e., the Nile - forth from his course; the light shineth upon thy body and thou art the dweller in Nekhen.[49] Oh, grant thou unto me a path whereon I may pass in peace, for I am just and true; I have not spoken lies wittingly, nor have I done aught with deceit."

"Homage to thee, O creator of the gods, thou King of the North and of the South, O Osiris, victorious one, ruler of the world in thy gracious seasons, thou art the lord of the celestial world.[50] Oh, grant thou unto me a path whereon I may pass in peace, for I am just and true! I have not spoken lies wittingly, nor have I done aught with deceit."

HYMN TO RA

(From the Papyrus of Ani, British Museum, No. 10,470, sheet 20)

A hymn of praise to Ra when he riseth in the eastern part of heaven. Those who are in his train rejoice, and lo! Osiris Ani, victorious saith:

"Hail thou Disk, thou lord of rays, who risest on the horizon day by day! Shine thou with thy beams of light upon the face of Osiris Ani, who is victorious; for he singeth hymns of praise unto thee at dawn, and he maketh thee to set at eventide with words of adoration. May the soul of Osiris Ani, the triumphant one, come forth with thee into heaven, may he go forth in the Mater boat. May he come into port in the Sekter boat, and may he cleave his path among the never-resting stars in the heavens."

Footnotes

36. The four pillars at the south, north, west, and east of heaven upon which the heavens were believed to rest.

37. Or, "I am at peace with the god of the city."

38. "Existence in Peace," the name of the first section of the Elysian Fields.

39. The name of a pool in the second section of the Elysian Fields.

40. The name of a pool in the first section of the Elysian Fields.

41. He name of a pool in the second section of the Elysian Fields.

42. The name of a district in the third section of the Elysian Fields.

43. The name of a pool In the first section of the Elysian Fields.

44. "Usert," the name of a pool in the third section of the Elysian Fields.

45. "Smam," the name of a pool in the third section of the Elysian Fields.

46. A name of the city of Mendes, the metropolis of the sixteenth nome of Lower Egypt.

47. "He ate his heart." He lost his temper and raged.

48. "The place where nothing groweth," the name of a district in the underworld.

49. The name of the sanctuary of the goddess Nekhebet in Upper Egypt.
50. The two lands, Atebui, which were situated one on each side of the celestial Nile.

CHAPTER V

HERMES TRISMEGISTUS

Hermes Trismegistus, "the thrice greatest Hermes." The name given by the Greeks to the Egyptian god Thoth or Tehuti, the god of wisdom, learning, and literature. Thoth is alluded to in later Egyptian writings as "twice very great" and even as "five times very great" in some demotic or popular scripts. - ca. third century B.C. To him was attributed as "scribe of the gods" the authorship of all sacred books which were thus called "Hermetic" by the Greeks. These, according to Clemens Alexandrinus, were forty-two in number and were sub-divided into six portions, of which the first dealt with priestly education, the second with temple ritual, and the third with geographical matter. The fourth division treated of astrology, the fifth of hymns in honor of the gods and a text-book for the guidance of Kings, while the sixth was medical. It is unlikely that these books were all the work of one individual, and it is more probable that they represent the accumulated wisdom of Egypt, attributed in the course of ages to the great god of wisdom.

As "scribe of the gods" Thoth was also the author of all strictly sacred writing. Hence by a convenient fiction the name of Hermes was placed at the head of an extensive cycle of mystic literature, produced in post-Christian times. Most of this Hermetic or Trismegistic literature has perished, but all that remains of it has been gathered and translated into English. It includes the "Poimandres" - virgin of the world - , "the Perfect Sermon," or the "Asclepius" excerpts by Stobacus, and fragments from the church fathers and from the philosophers, Zosimus and Fulgentius. Hitherto these writings have been neglected by theologians, who have dismissed them as the offspring of third century Neo-Platoism. According to the generally accepted view they were eclectic compilations, combining neo-Platonic philosophy, Philonic Judaism and Kabalistic theosophy in an attempt to supply a philosophic substitute for Christianity. The many Christian elements to be found in these mystic scriptures were ascribed to plagiarism. By an examination of early mystery writings and traditions it has been proved with some degree of certainty that the main source of Trismegistic Tractates is the wisdom of Egypt, and that they "go back in an unbroken tradition of type and form and context to the earliest Ptolemaic times."

The "Poimandres," on which all later Trismegistic literature is based, must, at least in its original form, be placed not later than the first century. The charge of plagiarism from Christian writings, therefore, falls to the ground. If it can be proved that the "Poimandres" belongs to the first century, we have in it a valuable document in determining the environment and development of Christian origins.

Mr. G. R. S. Mead, author of "Thrice Greatest Hermes," says in an illuminating passage: "The more one studies the best of these mystical sermons, casting aside all prejudices, and trying to feel and think with the writers, the more one is conscious of approaching the threshold of what may well be believed to have been the true adytum. of the best in the mystery traditions of antiquity, Innumerable are the hints of the greatnesses and immensities lying beyond that threshold - among other precious things the vision of the key to Egypt's wisdom, the interpretation of apocalypsis by the light the sun-clear epopteia of the intelligible cosmos."

HERMETIC WRITINGS

Apparently the earliest of the Hermetic class of writings is the Kore Kosmou or Virgin of the World.

It has more connection with the earlier mythology of Egypt than the other works, Isis and Horus are the teacher and taught; Thoth, Imhotep, and Ptah are all named; the mission of Osiris and Isis is recounted; the divine parentage of the kings is described, and Egypt is the happy centre of all the world. As such Egyptian detail is absent from works of the first or second century B.C., it would be reasonable to put this earlier; and the Egyptian forms of the names of the gods imply earlier translation than that of the other works. What seems to stamp the period is an allusion in sect. 48, where the central land of Egypt is described as "free from trouble, ever it brings forth, adorns and educates, and only with such weapons wars - on men - and wins the victory, and with consummate skill, like a good satrap bestows the fruit of its own victory upon the vanquished." It would seem impossible for the allusion to the government of a satrap to be preferred by an Egyptian, except under the Persian dominion. And such a reference to wise government could not occur in the very troubled years of plunder and confusion, 342 to 332 B.C. We must go back to the days of wise and righteous rule of Persia, 525-405 B.C., to reach a possible comparison with the wise satrap. We know so little of the details of the Persian dealings with Egypt, that the allusion to a generous satrap can hardly be fixed in history. But it is probable that the reference is to the events of the conquest by Cambyses in 525, followed by the enlightened reign of Darius, beginning in 521, soon after which, about 518, the satrap Aryandes attacked Cyrene, and brought back much spoil of captives and plunder into Egypt. Thus within a few years of the conquest of Egypt, a good satrap bestowed the fruits of victory upon the vanquished. This would throw the Kore Kosmou back to about 510 B.C., but in any case we must, by this allusion to a satrap, date it with a century after that. Thus it would precede all the Apocryphal Wisdom literature of Alexandria, and indeed there is no trace of Jewish influence in the ideas or language.

THE SUBJECT OF THE WORK IS THE ORIGIN OF ALL THINGS

Beginning with the principle "that every nature which lies underneath should be co-ordered and fulfilled by those that lie above," this is carried out by the dive production of heavenly souls, and next of sacred animals. The souls rebel and are then embodied as men, and the gods form the world for them. The evils of man are righted by the Divine Efflux, Osiris and Isis, and the nature of man is explained. Such is the argument of the work, obscured by magnificent images and phrases. The various beliefs which are stated or implied give a body of ideas, which we can thus date as underlying the rest of the literature. The numbers here refer to Mead's sections.

In (1) we read of the divine beauty of the rich majesty of Night, before God was known, and of the ordered motions and hidden influences of the Sun and planets bestowing order on the things below. (2) Beside the Creator there were immortal gods, into whom he breathes love and pours radiance, that they might seek and desire to find and win success. (3) Among the gods were Hermes Tat his son and heir, afterwards came Asklepios-Imhotep according to the will of Ptah who is Hephaistos. Their inquiry was ordained by Fore-knowledge of Providence, queen of all; thus fate is over the gods. (5) Hermes binds his holy books with spells, until they shall be found by souls. (6) When the Kosmos was to awake, God said, "Nature, arise!" and from His word came a perfectly beautiful feminine principle, at whom the gods marvelled. This seems to be the Kore Kosmou or Virgin of the Kosmos, after whom this writing is named. By the help of Toil she made her daughter Invention, who was to rule over all that had been made. These, however, take no further action, but (8) the Breath of God and Conscious Fire blended with unconscious matter is (9) the material for myriads of souls (10) of sixty different degrees. (11) These kept the circulation of Nature in motion, but are threatened if they transgress. (12) God then makes the sacred animals of water and of earth, and gives some matter to the souls to make men in their own nature. The souls make birds of the lightest stuff, quadrupeds of the stiffer plasm, then fish, and of the cold and heavy residue creeping things. But the whole of this existence is entirely before and outside of the present world of men.

The second great stage is the rebellion of souls and its results. (15) Proud of their work, the souls armed themselves, and were forever moving; God therefore resolved to embody them as men. (16) The gods are called to promise their gifts to the new world of men. (17) The sun will shine; the moon give fear, silence, sleep and memory; Kronos will give justice and necessity; Zeus will give fortune, hope, and peace; Ares gives struggle, wrath and strife; Aphrodite gives despair, desire, bliss, and laughter; and Hermes gives prudence, wisdom, persuasiveness, and truth, and will work with invention. This idea of the gods endowing men is seen in the tale of the creation of the wife of Bata, and is therefore Egyptian, but the details are Greek in origin. It is possible that sect. 17 is a later Greek expansion inserted in the Egyptian text; otherwise we must regard the whole as a Græco-Egyptian philosophy, for the Egyptian would not admit Greek elements at this date into a religious myth.

(18) Hermes then made the bodies, with too much water added that they should not be powerful. The souls are thus enfleshed by God, and wail at their fate. (19) The history of this was confided by Hermes to Kneph, and by him told to Isis,

who now tells Horus. (20,21). The wail of imprisoned souls is (22) answered by God that if they are sinless they shall dwell in the fields of Heaven - fields of Aalu - , if blameable then on earth, if they improve they shall regain Heaven, but if they sin worse then they shall become animals. Here Metempsychosis is fully stated, as in Plato; but it is not in the Egyptian form, and the Indian influence appears already at work. (23) Then all receive breath, and the reward of the final dissolution of the body is a return to the happiness of their first state. The more righteous, upon the threshold of the divine change, shall be righteous kings, genuine philosophers, founders of states, lawgivers, real seers, true herb-knowers, prophets of the gods, skillful musicians, astronomers, augurers and sacrificers. (24) Others lower shall be eagles, lions, dragons and dolphins.

(25) Then a mighty spirit rises from the earth, and as the souls were entering their plasms he protests against making such daring and (26) enquiring beings, and (27) prays that they may have pain, cares, struggles, and illness to keep them down. This conception seems quite un-Egyptian, and much more of the Pandora type. (28) Hermes agrees to impose Fate upon them. (29) God then assembled the gods who are free from all decay and who regulate the mighty Aeon - the only æonic reference here - to join with him in making the Heaven, earth, and sun. All previous creations appear to have been pre-sensuous, the visible world only now appearing. (31) Then the souls cause such impious turmoil, newly shut in prison, that (32) Fire complains that it is turned from sacrificial rites with sweet-smelling vapours, to burn up flesh - this point is strongly Indian, as implying that no flesh was sacrificed, but only spices - ; (33) Air complains that it is polluted with dead bodies, Water complains that rivers wash the hands of murderers and receive the slain; and (34) Earth complains that it is dishonoured by the corruption of their carcases. (35) God remedies this condition by sending another efflux of His nature. (36) Osiris and Isis. They filled life full of life, stopped slaughter, hallowed shrines, gave laws, food, and shelter, set up courts of law, filled the world with justice, and introduced the witness of an oath. They also taught embalming, and the doctrine of the soul passing out in a swoon - which might result in death - taught about daimons, and engraved the teaching, were authors of arts, sciences, and laws, established the sacred rites, the grade of prophets, and magic, philosophy, and medicine. This is far earlier than the account of Osiris by Plutarch, and agrees with that. (38) Then Osiris and Isis, having fulfilled their mission, were demanded back by those who dwell in Heaven, and were permitted to return.

HORUS DEMANDS HOW ROYAL SOULS ARE BORN

Isis replies that in Heaven the gods dwell with the Architect of all, in the Aether are the stars and the sun, in the Air are souls and the moon, and on Earth are men and living things. (40) The king is the last of gods but first of men, divorced from his godship while on earth; his soul descends from a region above that of other souls. (41) Those who have lived a blameless life and are about to be changed into gods, become kings that they may train for godship; or those souls who are already gods, but have slightly erred, are born as kings. (42) Dispositions of kings depend upon their angels and daimons who attend them. (43) The birth of noble souls is because they descend from a more glorious place - agreeing with the idea of sixty grades of souls - . (44) Sex is a thing of bodies not of souls. (46) The inhabited earth is like a human being lying face up, (47) at the south is its head, its feet at the north; on the right to the east are fighters, on the left to the west men fight with the left hand, those to the north excel in legs and feet. Egypt is the heart, its men gifted with intelligence and filled with wisdom. (48) The Nile flows from the south on breaking of the frost; east and west is burnt by the rising and setting sun, and the north congealed. Hence Egypt alone is happy. (49, 50) Souls are constrained differently by the four elements.

The most essential notions that we see here are creation by the word, the gods acting under the command of a supreme God, the function of created souls to keep nature circulating, the body a prison of the soul, the heavenly types of animals preceding the earthly creation, and the mission of gods on earth. Besides the Egyptian ideas already mentioned, Greek influence is seen in the characters of gods and in the episode of the earth spirit, and probably Indian influence in the Metempsychosis and the fire-sacrifice of spices, as by Apollonios. There is throughout this cosmology a vigorous and eventful chain of thought, entirely different to the maundering of later writers.

Closely linked with the Kore Kosmou is the sermon of Isis to Horus. It is slightly less Egyptian, writing of Hephaistos and Ptah, classing Horus with the mighty gods, and being rather less concrete. It may then be a rather later continuation, as it closely joins on in subject to the close of the Kore Kosmou. The ideas of this sermon are that the souls of men and animals are all alike, and Metempsychosis is assumed between human and animal bodies; the soul is individual, the work of God's hands and mind; its congress with the body is a concord wrought by God's necessity; at death it returns to its proper region. The reign of souls is between the moon and earth, for above the moon are the gods and stars and providence; the souls pass through air and wind without friction; their reign is divided into the four quarters of earth, higher the eight winds, higher sixteen spaces of subtler air, and highest thirty-two spaces of subtlest air; these are called zones, firmaments, or strata. The kingly souls occupy the highest, and so in order down to the base souls the lowest. There is a warder of souls, and a conductor to and from the bodies. Bodies are a blend of the four elements, each affecting the character.

THE VIRGIN OF THE WORLD

"From Thrice Greatest Hermes' sacred book 'The Virgin of the World.'"

1. So speaking Isis doth pour forth for Horus the sweet draught - the first - of deathless which souls have custom to receive from gods, and thus begins her holiest discourse - logos - .

Seeing that, Son Horus, Heaven, adorned with many a wreath - of starry crowns - , is set o'er every nature of - all - things beneath, and that nowhere it lacketh aught of anything which the whole cosmos now doth hold, - in every way it needs must be that every nature which lies underneath, should be co-ordered and full-filled by those that lie above; for things below cannot of course give order to the ordering above.

It needs must, therefore, be the less should give place to the greater mysteries. The ordinance of the sublimer things transcends the lower; it is both sure in every way and falleth 'neath no mortal's thought. Wherefore the - mysteries - below did sign, fearing the wondrous beauty and the everlasting durance of the ones above.

'Twas worth the gazing and the pains to see Heaven's beauty, beauty that seemed like God, -

God who was yet unknown, and the rich majesty of night, who weaves her web with rapid light, though it be less than sun's, and of the other mysteries in turn that move in Heaven, with ordered motions and with periods of times, with certain hidden influences bestowing order on the things below and co-increasing them.

2. Thus fear succeeded fear, and searching search incessant, and for so long as the Creator of the universals willed, did ignorance retain its grip on all. But when He judged it fit to manifest Him who He is, He breathed into the Gods and Loves, and freely poured the splendor which He had within His heart, into their minds, in ever greater and still greater measure; that firstly they might have the wish to seek, next they might yearn to find, and finally have power to win success as well. But this, my Horus, wonder-worthy son, could never have been done had that seed been subject to death, for that as yet had no existence, but only with a soul that could vibrate responsive to the mysteries of Heaven.

3. Such was all-knowing Hermes, who saw all things, and seeing understood, and understanding had the power both to disclose and to give explanation. For what he knew, he graved on stone; yet though he graved them onto stone he hid them mostly, keeping sure silence though in speech, that every younger age of cosmic time might seek for them. And thus, with charge unto his kinsmen of the Gods to keep sure watch, he mounted to the stars.

To him succeeded Tat, who was at once his son and heir unto these knowledges; and not long afterwards Asclepius-Imuth, according to the will of Ptah who is Hephæstus, and all the rest who were to make enquiry of the faithful certitude of heavenly contemplation, as foreknowledge willed, foreknowledge queen of all.

4. Hermes, however, made explanation to surrounding - space - , how that not even to his son - because of the yet newness of his youth - had he been able to hand on the Perfect Vision. But when the sun did rise for me, and with all-seeing eyes I gazed upon the hidden - mysteries - of that new dawn, and contemplated

them, slowly there came to me - but it was sure - conviction that the sacred symbols of the cosmic elements were hid away hard by the secrets of Osiris.

5. - Hermes - , ere he returned to Heaven, invoked a spell on them, and spake these words. - For 'tis not meet, my son, that I should leave this proclamation ineffectual, but - rather - should speak forth what words - our - Hermes uttered when he hid his books away. Thus then he said:

"O holy books, who have been made by my immortal hands, by incorruption's magic spells. . . . free from decay and incorrupt from time! Become unseeable, for every one whose foot shall tread the plains of this - our - land, until old Heaven doth bring forth meet instruments for you, whom the Creator shall call souls."

Thus spake he, and, laying spells on them by means of his own works, he shuts them safe away in their own zones. And long enough the time has been since they were hid away.

6. And Nature, O my son, was barren, till they who then were under orders to patrol the Heaven, approaching to the God of all, their King, reported on the lethargy of things. The time was come for cosmos to awake, and this was no one's task but His alone.

"We pray Thee, then," they said, "direct Thy thought to things which now exist and to what things the future needs."

7. When they spake thus, God smiled and said: "Nature, arise!" And from His word there came a marvel, feminine, possessed of perfect beauty, gazing at which the Gods stood all-amazed. And God the Fore-father, with name of Nature, honoured her, and bade her be prolific.

Then gazing fixedly on the surrounding space, He spake these words as well: "Let Heaven be filled with all things full, and Air, and Æther too!" God spake and it was so. And Nature with herself communing knew she must not disregard the Sire's command; so with the help of Toil she made a daughter fair, whom she did call Invention. And on her God bestowed the gift of being, and with His gift He set apart all them that had been so-far made, filled them with mysteries, and to Invention gave the power of ruling them.

8. But He, no longer willing that the world above should be inert, but think good to fill it full of breaths, so that its parts should not remain immotive and inert, He thus began on these with use of holy arts as proper for the bringing forth of His own special work.

For taking breath from His own breath and blending this with knowing Fire, He mingled them with certain other substances which have no power to know; and having made the two - either with other one, with certain hidden words of power, He thus set all the mixture going thoroughly; until out of the compost smiled a substance, as it were, far subtler, purer far, and more translucent than the things from which it came; it was so clear that no one but the artist could detect it.

9. And since it neither thawed when fire was set unto it - for it was made of fire - , nor yet did freeze when it had once been properly produced - for it

was made of breath - , but it kept its mixture's composition a certain special kind, peculiar to itself, of special type and special blend, - which composition, you must know, God called psychosis, after the more auspicious meaning of the name and from the similarity of its behaviour - it was from this coagulate He fashioned souls enough in myriads, moulding with order and with measure the efflorescent product of the mixture for what He willed, with skilled experience and fitting reason, so that they should not be compelled to differ any way one from another.

10. For, you must know the efflorescence that exhaled out of the movement God induced, was not like to itself. For that its first florescence was greater, fuller, every way more pure, than was its second; its second was far second to the first, but greater far than this was its third. And thus the total number of degrees reached up to sixty. In spite of this, in laying down the law, He ordered it that all should be eternal, as though from out one essence, the forms of which Himself alone could bring to their completion.

11. Moreover, He appointed for them limits and reservations in the height of upper Nature, that they might keep the cylinder a-whirl in proper order and economy and - thus - might please their Sire. And so in that all-fairest station of the Æther He summoned unto Him the natures of all things that had as yet been made, and spake these words:

"O Souls, ye children fair of Mine own breath and My solicitude, whom I have now with My own hands brought to successful birth and consecrate to My own world, give ear unto these words of Mine as unto laws, and meddle not with any other space but that which is appointed for you by My will.

"For you, if ye keep steadfast, the Heaven, with the star-order, and thrones I have ordained fullfilled with virtue, shall stay as now they are for you; but if ye shall in any way attempt some innovation contrary to My decrees, I swear to you by My most holy breath, and by this mixture out of which I brought you into being, and by these hands of Mine which gave you life, that I will speedily devise for you a bond and punishments."

12. And having said these words, the God, who is my Lord, mixed the remaining cognate elements - water and earth - together, and, as before, invoking on them certain occult words, words of great power though not so potent as the first, He set them moving rapidly, and breathed into the mixture power of life; and taking the coagulate - which like the other floated to the top - , when it had been well steeped and had become consistent, He modelled out of it those of the - sacred animals possessing forms like unto men's.

The mixtures' residue He gave unto those souls that had gone in advance and had been summoned to the lands of gods, to regions near the stars, and to the - choir of - holy daimons. He said:

13. "My sons, ye children of My Nature, fashion things! Take ye the residue of what My art hath made, and let each fashion something which shall bear

resemblance to his own nature. These will I further give to you as models."

He took and set in order fair and fine, agreeably to the motions of the souls, the world of sacred animals, appending as it were to those resembling men those which came next in order, and on these types of lives He did bestow the all devising powers and all-contriving pro-creative breath of all the things which were for ever generally to be.

And He withdrew, with promises to join unto the visible productions of their hands breath that cannot be seen, and essence of engendering its like to each, so that they might give birth to others like themselves. And these are under no necessity to do aught else than what they did at first.

14. - And Horus asked - :

What did the souls do, Mother, then?

And Isis said:

Taking the blend of matter, Horus, my son, they first looked at the Father's mixture and adored it, and tried to find out whence it was composed; but this was not an easy thing for them to know.

They then began to fear lest they should fall beneath the Father's wrath for trying to find out, and so they set to work to do what they were bid.

Thereon, out of the upper stuff which had its topmost layer superfluously light, they formed the race of birds; while they were doing this the mixture had become half hardened, and by this time had taken on a firm consistency - thereon they fashioned out the race of things which have four feet - next they did fashion forth - the race of fish—less light and needing a moist substance of a different kind to swim in; and as the residue was of a cold and heavy nature, from it the Souls devised the race of creeping things.

15. They then, my son, as though they had done something grand, with overbusy daring armed themselves, and acted contrary to the commands they had received; and forthwith they began to overstep their proper limits and their reservations, and would no longer stay in the same place, but were forever moving, and thought that being ever stationed in one place was death.

That they would do this thing, however, O my son - as Hermes says when he speaks unto me - , had not escaped the eye of Him who is the God and Lord of universal things; and He searched out a punishment and bond, the which they now in misery endure.

Thus was it that the Sovereign King of all resolved to fabricate with art the human frame, in order that in it the race of souls throughout might be chastised.

16. "Then sending for me," Hermes says, "He spake: 'Soul of My Soul, and holy mind of My own Mind, up to what point, the nature of the things beneath, shall be seen in the gloom? How long shall what has up to now been made remain inactive and be destitute of praise? Bring hither to Me now, My son, all of the Gods in heaven,' said God" - as Hermes saith.

And when they came obedient to His command, - "Look down," said He, "upon the earth, and all beneath." And they forthwith both looked and understood the Sovereign's will. And when He spake to them on human kind's behalf, they - all - agreed to furnish those who were to be, with whatsoever thing they each could best provide.

17. Sun said: "I'll shine unto my full." Moon promised to pour light upon the after-the-sun course, and said she had already given birth to fear and silence, and also sleep, and memory - a thing that would turn out to be most useful to them.

Cronus announced himself already sire of justice and necessity.

Zeus said: "So that the race which is to be may not forever fight, already for them have I made fortune, and hope and peace."

Ares declared he had become already sire of struggle, wrath, and strife.

Nor yet did Aphrodite hesitate; she also said: "I'll join to them desire, my Lord, and bliss, and laughter - too - , so that our kindred souls, in working out their very grievous condemnation, may not exhaust their punishment unto the full."

Full pleased were all, my son, at Aphrodite's words.

"And for my part," said Hermes, "I will make men's nature well endowed; I will devote to them prudence and wisdom, persuasiveness and truth, and never will I cease from congress with invention, but ever will I benefit the mortal life of men born underneath my types of life. For that the types our Father and Creator hath set apart for me, are types of wisdom and intelligence, and more than ever - is this so - what time the motion of the stars set over them doth have the natural power of each consonant with itself."

18. And God, the Master of the universe, rejoiced on hearing this, and ordered that the race of men should be.

"I," Hermes says, "was seeking for the stuff which had to be employed, and calling on the Monarch for His aid. And He gave order to the souls to give the mixture's residue; and taking it I found it utterly dried up.

"Thereon, in mixing it, I used more water far than was required to bring the matter back unto its former state, so that the plasm was in every way relaxable, and weak and powerless, in order that it might not in addition to its natural sagacity, be full of power as well.

"I moulded it, and it was fair; and I rejoiced at seeing mine own work, and from below I called upon the Monarch to behold. And He did look on it, and was rejoiced, and ordered that the souls should be enfleshed.

"Then were they first plunged in deep gloom, and, learning that they were condemned, began to wail. I was myself amazed at the souls' utterances."

19. Now give good heed, son Horus, for thou are being told the mystic spectacle which Kamephis, our forefather, was privileged to hear from Hermes, record-writer of all deeds, and I from Kamephis, most ancient of - us - all, when he did honour me with the black - rite - that gives perfection; hear thou it now from me.

For when, O wondrous Sun of mighty fame, they were about to be shut in their prisons, some simply uttered wails and groans - in just the selfsame way as beasts that once have been a liberty, when torn from their accustomed haunts they love so well, will be bad slaves, will fight and make revolt, and be in no agreement with their masters; nay more, if circumstances should serve, will even do to death those that oppress them.

Others with louder outcry hissed like snakes; another shrieked shrilly, and ere he spake shed many tears, and, turning up and down what things served him as eyes, he said:

20. "O Heaven, thou source of our begetting, O Æther, air, O hands and holy breath of God our Monarch, O ye most brilliant stars, eyes of the gods, O tireless light of sun and moon, co-nurslings of our origin, - reft from (you) all we suffer piteously.

"And this the more, in that from spacious realms of light, from out - thy - holy envelope and wealthy dome, and from the blessed government we shared with gods, we shall be thus shut down into these honourless and lowly quarters.

"What is the so unseemly thing we miserables have done? What - crime - deserves these punishments? How many sins await us wretched ones? How many are the things we have to do in this our hopeless plight, necessities to furnish for this watery frame that is soon dissolved?

21. "For that no longer shall our eyes behold the souls of God; when through such watery spheres as these we see our own forefather Heaven grown small and tiny, we shall dissolve in signs, - nay, there'll be times we shall not see at all, for sentence hath been passed on us poor things; the gift of real sight hath not been given to us, in that it hath not been permitted us to see without the light. Windows, they are, not eyes!

"How wretchedly shall we endure to hear our kindred breaths breathe in the air, when we no longer shall be breathing with them! For home, instead of this great world high in the air, a heart's small mass awaits us. Set Thou us free from bonds so base as these to which we have sunk down, and end our grief!

"O Lord and Father, and our Maker, if so it be Thou hast thus quickly grown indifferent unto the works of Thine own Hands, appoint for us some limits! Still deem us worthy of some words, though they be few, while yet we can see through the whole world-order bright on every side."

22. Thus speaking, Horus, son, the Souls gained their request; for that the Monarch came, and sitting on the throne of truth made answer to their prayers:

"O souls, love and Necessity shall be your lords, they who are lords and marshals after Me of all. Know, all of you who are set under My gaining rule, that as long as ye keep you free of sin, ye shall dwell in the fields of Heaven; but if some cause of blame for aught attached itself to you, ye shall dwell in the place that Destiny allots, condemned to mortal wombs.

"If, then, the things imputed to your charge be slight, leaving the bond of fleshly frames subject to death, ye shall again embrace your - father - Heaven, and sin no more; but if ye shall commit some greater sins, and with the end appointed of your frames be not advanced, no longer shall ye dwell in Heaven, nor even in the bodies of mankind, but shall continue after that to wander round in lives irrational."

23. Thus speaking, Horus mine, He gave to all the gift of breath, and thus continued:

"It is not without purpose or by chance I have laid down the law of your transformings; but as - it will be - for the worse if ye do aught unseemly, so for the better, if she shall will what's worthy of your birth.

"For L and no one else, will be the witness and the watcher. Know, then, it is for what ye have done heretofore, ye do endure this being shut in bodies as a punishment.

"The difference in your rebirths, accordingly, for you, shall be as I have said, a difference of bodies, and their - final - dissolution - shall be - a benefit and a - return to - the fair happiness of former days.

"But if ye think to do aught else unworthy of Me, your mind shall lose its sight so as to think the contrary - of what is true - , and take the punishment for benefit; the change to better things for infamous despite.

"But the more righteous of you, who stand upon the threshold of the change to the diviner state, shall among men be righteous kings, and genuine philosophers, founders of states, and lawgivers, and real seers, and true herb-knowers, and prophets of the gods most excellent, skillful musicians, skilled astronomers, and augurs wise, consummate sacrificers - as many of you as are worthy of things fair and good.

24. "Among winged tribes - they shall be - eagles, for these will neither scare away their kind nor feed on them; nay more, when they are by, no other weaker beast will be allowed by them to suffer wrong, for what will be the eagles' nature is too just - to suffer it - .

"Among four-footed things - they will be - lions, - a life of strength and of a kind which in a measure needs no sleep, in mortal body practising the exercises of immortal life - for they nor weary grow nor sleep.

"And among creeping things - they will be - dragons, in that this animal will have great strength and live for long, will do no harm, and in a way be friends with man, and let itself be tamed; it will possess no poison and will cast its skin, as the nature of the Gods.

"Among the things that swim - they will be - dolphins; for dolphins will take pity upon those who fall into the sea, and if they are still breathing bear them to the land, while if they're dead they will not ever even touch them, though they will be the most voracious tribe that in the water dwells."

25. Thus speaking God became imperishable mind. Thereon, son Horus, from earth uprose a very mighty spirit which no mass of body could contain,

whose strength consisted in his intellect. And though he knew full well the things on which he questioned - the body with which man was clothed according to his type, a body fair and dignified, yet savage overmuch and full of fear - immediately he saw the souls were entering the plasms, he cried out:

"What are these called, O Hermes, writer of the records of the gods?"

And when He answered "Men!" - " Hermes," he said, "it is a daring work, this making man, with eyes inquisitive, and talkative of tongue, with power henceforth to hear things even which are no concern of his, dainty of smell, who will use to its full his power of touch on every thing.

"Hast thou, his generator, judged it good to leave him from care, who in the future daringly will gaze upon the fairest mysteries which Nature hath? Wouldst thou leave him without a grief, who in the days to come will make his thoughts reach unto mysteries beyond the Earth?

26. "Men will dig up the roots of plants, and will find out their juices' qualities. Men will observe the nature of the stones. Men will dissect not only animals irrational, but they'll dissect themselves, daring to find out how they were made. They will stretch out their daring hands e'en to the sea, and cutting self-grown forests down will ferry one another o'er to lands beyond. - Men - will seek out as well the inner nature of the holy spaces which no foot may tread, and will chase after them into the great Space, desiring to observe the nature of the motion of the Heaven.

"These are yet moderate things - which they will do - . For nothing more remains than earth's remotest realms; nay, in their daring they will track out night, the farthest night of all.

27. "Naught have they, then, to stop them from receiving their initiation in the good of freedom from all pain, and unconstrained by terror's grievous goads, from living softly out a life free from care.

"Then will they not gird on the armour of an over-busy daring up to Heaven? Will they not, then, reach out their souls free from all care unto the - primal - elements themselves?

"Teach them henceforth to long to plan out something, where they have as well to fear the danger of its ill-success, in order that they may be tamed by the sharp tooth of pain in failure of their hopes.

"Let the too busy nature of their souls be balanced by desires, and fears, and griefs, and empty hopes.

"Let loves in quick succession sway their souls, hopes, manifold desires, sometimes fulfilled, and sometimes unfulfilled, that the sweet bait of their success may draw them into struggle amid direr ills,

"Let fever lay its heavy hand on them, that losing heart they may submit desire to discipline."

28. Thou grievest, dost thou, Horus, Son, to hear thy mother put these things in words? Art thou not struck with wonder, art thou not terrorstruck at how poor

man was grievously oppressed? Hear what is sadder still!

When Momos said these things Hermes was pleased, for what he said was said out of affection for him; and so he did all that he recommended, speaking thus:

"Momos, the nature of the breath divine which doth surround - all things - shall not become inert. The Master of the universe appointed me as steward and as manager.

Wherefore the overseer of His command will be the keen-eyed goddess of the all, Adrasteia; and I will skillfully devise an instrument, mysterious, possessed of power of sight that cannot err, and cannot be escaped, whereto all things on earth shall of necessity be subject, from birth to final dissolution, - an instrument which binds together all that's done. This instrument shall rule all other things on earth as well - as man."

29. These words, said Hermes, did I speak to Momos, and forthwith the instrument was set a-going.

When this was done, and when the souls had entered in the bodies, and - Hermes - had himself been praised for what was done, again the Monarch did convoke the gods in session. The gods assembled, and once more did He make proclamation, saying:

"Ye Gods, all ye who have been made of chiefest nature, free from all decay, who have received as your appointed lot for ever more to order out the mighty Aeon, through whom all universal things will never weary grow surrendering themselves in urn the one to other, - how long shall we be rulers of this sovereignty that none can ever know? How long these things, shall they transcend the power of sight of sun and moon?

"Let each of us bring forth according to his power. Let us by our own energy wipe out this inert state of things; let chaos seem to be a myth incredible to future days. Set hand to mighty work; and I myself will first begin."

30. He spake; straightway in cosmic order there began the differentiation of the up-to-then black unity - of things - . And heaven shone forth above tricked out with all his mysteries; earth, still a-tremble, as the sun shone forth grew harder, and appeared with all the fair adornment that bedeck her round on every side. For beautiful to God are even things which men think mean, in that in truth they have been made to serve the laws of God.

And God rejoiced when now He saw His works a-moving; and filling full His hands, which held as much as all surrounding space, with all that nature had produced, and squeezing tight the handfuls mightily, He said:

"Take - these - , O holy Earth, take those, all honoured one, who are to be the mother of all things, and henceforth lack thou naught!"

31. God spake and opening His hands, such hands as God should have, He poured them all into the composition of the world. And they in the beginning were unknown in every way; for that the souls as newly shut in prison, not

enduring their disgrace, began to strive in emulation with the gods in heaven, in full command, in that they had the same creator, made revolt, and using weaker men as instruments, began to make them set upon each other, and range themselves in conflict, and make war among themselves.

Thus strength did mightily prevail o'er weakness, so that the strong did burn and massacre the weak, and from the holy places down they cast the living and the dead down from the holy shrines, until the elements in their distress resolved to go to God their Monarch - to complain - about the savage state in which men lived.

The evil now being very great, the elements approached to God who made them, and formulated their complaint in some such words as these:

32. It was moreover fire who first received authority to speak. He said:

"O Lord, artificer of this new world, thou name mysterious among the gods, and up to now revered by all mankind, how long hast Thou, O Daimon, judged it right to leave the life of mortals without God?

"Show now Thyself unto Thy world consulting Thee; initiate the savagery of life with peace; give laws to life; to right give oracles; fill with fair hopes all things; and let men fear the vengeance of the gods, and none will sin.

"Should they receive due retribution for their sins, they will refrain henceforth from doing wrong; they will respect their oaths, and no one any more will ponder sacrilege.

"Let them be taught to render thanks for benefits received, that I, the fire, may joyfully do service in the sacrificial rites, that they may from the altar send sweet-smelling vapours forth.

"For up to now I am polluted, Lord; and by the godless daring of these men I am compelled to burn up flesh. They will not let me be for what I was brought forth; but they adulterate with all indecency my undecaying state."

33. And the air too said:

"I also, Master, I am made turbid by the vapours which the bodies of the dead exhale, and I am pestilential, and, no longer filled with health, I gaze down on things I ought not to behold."

Next water, O my son of mighty soul, received authority to speak, and spake and said:

"O Father, O wonderful creator of all things, daimon self-born, and Nature's maker, who through Thee doth conceive all things, now at this last, command the rivers' streams for ever to be pure, for that the rivers and the seas or wash the murderers' hands or else receive the murdered."

34. After came earth in bitter grief, and taking up the tale, O son of high renown, thus she began to speak:

"O sovereign Lord, chief of the heavenly ones, and master of the wheels, Thou ruler of us elements, O Sire of them who stand beside Thee, for whom all things have the beginning of their increase and of their decrease, and into whom they cease again and have the end that is their due according to necessity's decree, O greatly honoured One, the godless rout of men doth dance upon my bosom.

"I hold in my embrace as well as the nature of all things; for I, as Thou didst give command, not only bear them all, but I receive them also when they're killed. But now I am dishonoured. The world upon the earth though filled with all things - else - hath not a God.

"For having naught to fear they sin in everything, and from my heights, O Lord, down - dead - they fall from every evil art. And soaking with the juices of their carcases I'm all corrupt. Hence am I, Lord, compelled to hold in me those of no worth. With all I bear I would hold God as well.

"Bestow on earth, if not Thyself, for I could not contain Thee, yet some holy emanation of Thyself. Make Thou the earth more honoured than the rest of elements; for it is right that she should boast of gifts from Thee, in that she giveth all."

35. Thus spake the elements; and God, fulfilling all things with the sound of His - most - holy Voice, spake thus:

"Depart, ye Holy Ones, ye children worthy of a mighty sire, nor yet in any way attempt to innovate, nor leave the whole of - this - My world without your active service.

"For now another efflux of My nature is among you, and he shall be a pious supervisor of all deeds - judge incorruptible of living men and monarch absolute of those beneath the earth, not only striking terror - into them - but taking vengeance on them. And by his class of birth the fate he hath deserved shall follow every man."

And so the elements did cease from their complaint, upon the master's order, and they held their peace; and each of them continued in the exercise of his authority and in his rule.

36. And Horus thereon said:

How was it, mother, then, that earth received God's efflux?

And Isis said:

I may not tell the story of - this - birth; for it is not permitted to describe the origin of thy descent, O Horus - son - of mighty power, lest afterwards the way-of-birth of the immortal Gods should be known unto men, - except so far that God the monarch, the universal orderer and architect, sent for a little while thy mighty sire Osiris, and the mightiest [Goddess Isis, that they might help the world, for all things needed them.

'Tis they who filled life full of life. 'Tis they who caused the savagery of mutual slaughtering of men to cease. 'Tis they who hallowed precincts to the gods their ancestors and spots for holy rites. 'Tis they who gave to men laws, food, and shelter.

'Tis they who will, says Hermes, learn to know the secrets of my records all, and will make separation of them; and some they will keep for themselves, while those that are best suited for the benefit of mortal men, they will engrave on tablet and on obelisk.

'Tis they who were the first to set up courts of law; and filled the world with justice and fair rule. 'Tis they who were the authors of good pledges and of faith, and brought the mighty witness of an oath into men's lives.

'Tis they who taught men how to wrap up those who ceased to live, as they should be.

'Tis they who searched into the cruelty of death, and learned that though the spirit which goes out longs to return into men's bodies, yet if it ever fail to have the power of getting back again, then loss of life results.

'Tis they who learned from Hermes that surrounding space was filled with daimons, and graved on hidden stones - the hidden teaching - .

'Tis they alone who, taught by Hermes in God's hidden codes, became the authors of the arts, and sciences, and all pursuits which men do practice, and givers of the laws.

'Tis they who, taught by Hermes that the things below have been disposed of by God to be in sympathy with things above, established on the earth the sacred rites o'er which the mysteries in Heaven preside.

'Tis they who, knowing the destructibility of - mortal - frames, devised the grade of prophets, in all things perfected, in order that no prophet who stretched forth his hands unto the Gods, should be in ignorance of anything, that magic and philosophy should feed the soul, and medicine preserve the body when it suffered pain.

38. And having done all this, my son, Osiris and myself perceiving that the world was - now - quite full, were thereupon demanded back by those who dwell in Heaven, but could not go above until he had made appeal unto the monarch, that surrounding space might with this knowledge of the soul be filled as well, and we ourselves succeed in making our ascent acceptable - to Him - . . . For that God doth in hymns rejoice.

Ay, mother, Horus said. On me as well bestow the knowledge of this hymn, that I may not remain in ignorance.

And Isis said: Give ear, O son!

THE VIRGIN OF THE WORLD - II

39. Now if thou wouldst, O son of mighty soul, know aught beside, ask on!

And Horus said: O mother of great honour, I would know how royal souls are born?

And Isis said: Son Horus, the distinction which marks out the royal souls is somewhat of this kind.

Four regions are there in the universe which fall beneath a law and leadership which cannot be transgressed - heaven, and the æther, and the air, and the most holy earth.

Above in Heaven, son, the gods do dwell, o'er whom with all the rest doth rule the Architect of all; and in the æther - dwell - the stars o'er whom the mighty light-giver the sun holds sway; but in the air - live - only souls, o'er whom doth rule the moon; and on the earth - do dwell - men and the rest of living things, o'er whom he who doth happen to be king holds sway.

40. The gods engender, son, the kings it has deserved, to rule - the race - that lives on earth. The rulers are the emanations of the king, of whom the nearer to him is more royal than the rest; for that the sun, in that 'tis nearer than the moon to God, is far more vast and potent, to whom the moon comes second both in rank and power.

The king, then, is the last of all the other gods, but first of men; and so long as he is upon the earth, he is divorced from his true godship, but hath something that doth distinguish him from men and which is like to God.

The soul which is sent down to dwell in him, is from that space which is above those regions whence - the souls - descend to other men. Down from that space the souls are sent to rule for those two reasons, son.

41. They who have run a noble, blameless race throughout the cycle of their lives, and are about to be changed into Gods - are born as kings - in order that by exercise of kingship they may train themselves to use the power the gods enjoy; while certain souls who are already gods, but have in some slight way infringed the rule of life which God inspired, are born as kings, in order that they may not, in being clothed in bodies, undergo the punishment of loss of dignity as well as nature, and that they may not, when they are enfleshed, have the same lot as other men, but have when bound what they enjoyed when free.

42. The differences which are, however, in the dispositions shown by those who play the part of kings, are not determined by distinguishing their souls, for these are all divine, but by the constitution of the angels and the daimons who attend on them. For that such souls as these descending for such purposes do not come down without a guard and escort, for justice up above knows how to give to each what is its due estate e'en though they be made exiles from their country ever fair.

When, then, my son, the angels and the daimons who bring down the soul are of a warlike kind, it has to keep firm hold of their proclivities, forgetting its own proper deeds, but all the more remembering the doings of the other host attached to it.

When they are peaceful, then the soul as well doth order its own course in peace.

When they love justice, then it too defends the right.

When they are music-lovers, then it also sings.

And when they are truth-lovers, then it also doth philosophise.

For as it were out of necessity these souls keep a firm hold of the proclivities of those that bring them here; for they are falling down to man's estate, forgetting their own nature, and the farther they depart from it, the more they have in memory the disposition of those - powers - which shut them - into bodies - .

43. Well hast thou, mother, all explained, said Horus. But noble souls, - how they are born, thou hast not told me yet.

As on earth, son Horus, there are states which differ one from other, so also is it in the case of souls. For they have regions whence they start; and that which starts from a more glorious place, hath nobler birth than one which doth not so. For just as among men the free is thought more noble than the slave - for that which is superior in souls and of a ruling nature of necessity subjects what is inferior - so also, son . . .

44. And how are male and female souls produced?

Souls, Horus, son, are of the self-same nature in themselves, in that they are from one and the same place where the Creator modeled them; nor male nor female are they. Sex is a thing of bodies, not of souls.

That which brings it about that some of them are stouter, some more delicate, is, son, that - cosmic - "air" in which all things are made. "Air" for the soul is nothing but the body which envelops it, an element which is composed of earth and water, air and fire.

As. then, the composition of the female ones has more of wet and cold, but less of dry and warm, accordingly the soul which is shut in a plasm of this kind becomes relaxed and delicate, just as the contrary is found to be in case of males.

For in their case there's more of dry and warm, and less of cold and wet; wherefore the souls in bodies such as these are sturdy and more active.

45. And bow do souls become intelligent, O mother mine?

And Isis answered:

The organ of the sight, my son, is swathed in wrappings. When these are dense and thick, the eye is dim, but when they're thin and light, then is the sight most keen. So also is it for the soul. For it as well has envelopes incorporal appropriate to it, just as it is itself incorporal. These envelopes are "airs" which are in us. When these are light and thin and clear, then is the soul intelligent, but, on the contrary, when they are dense and thick and turbid, then - the soul - , as in bad weather, sees not at distance but only things which lie about its feet.

46. And Horus said:

What is the reason, mother, that the men outside our holiest land are not so wise of mind as our compatriots?

And Isis said:

The earth lies in the middle of the universe upon her back, like to a human being, with eyes turned up to heaven, and portioned out into as many regions as there are limbs in man.

She turns her eyes to heaven as though to her own sire, that with his changes she may also bring about her own.

She hath her head set to the south of all, right shoulder to southeast, left shoulder to southwest; her feet below the Bear, right foot beneath its tail, left under its head; her thighs beneath those that succeed the Bear; her waist beneath the middle - stars - .

47. A sign of this is that men in the south, who dwell upon her head, are fine about the head and have good hair. Those in the east are ready for a fight and archer folk - for this pertains to the right hand.

Those in the west are steadier and for the most part fight with the left hand, and what is done by others with the right, they for their part attribute to the left.

Those beneath the Bear excel in feet and have especially good legs.

Those who come after them a little way, about the zone which is our present Italy, and Greece, they all have well made thighs and backs . . .

Moreover, all these - northern - parts being whiter than the rest bear whiter men upon them,

'But since the holiest land of our forebears lies in the midst of earth, and that the midst of a man's body serves as the precinct of the heart alone, and heart's the spot from which the soul doth start, the men of it not only have no less the other things which all the rest possess, but as a special thing are gifted with intelligence beyond all men and filled with wisdom, in that they are begotten and brought up above her heart.

48. Further, my son, the south being the receiver of the clouds which mass themselves together from the atmosphere . . .

For instance, it is just because there is this concentration of them in the south, that it is said our river doth flow thence, upon the breaking up of the frost there.

For whensoe'er a cloud descends, it turns the air about it into mist, and sends it downward in a kind of fog; and fog or mist is an impediment not only to the eyes, but also to the mind.

Whereas the east, O Horus, great in glory, in that 'tis thrown into confusion and made over-hot by the continual risings of the sun, and in like fashion too, the west, its opposite, in that it suffers the same things through its descents, afford the men born in them no conditions for clear observation. And Boreas with his concordant cold, together with their bodies doth congeal the minds of men as well.

Whereas the centre of all these being pure and undisturbed, foreknows both for itself and all that are in it. For, free from trouble, ever it brings forth, adorns and educates, and only with such weapons wars - on men - , and wins the victory, and with consummate skill, like a good satrap, bestows the fruit of its own victory upon the vanquished.

49. This too expound, O lady, mother of mine! For what cause is it that when men still keep alive in long disease, their rational part - their very reason and their very soul - at times becomes disabled?

And Isis answer made:

Of living things, my son, some are made friends with fire, and some with water, some with air, and some with earth, and some with two or three of these, and some with all.

And, on the contrary, again some are made enemies of fire, and some of water, some of earth, and some of air, and some of two of them, and some of three, and some of all.

For instance, son, the locust and all flies flee fire; the eagle and the hawk and all high-flying birds flee water; fish, air and earth; the snake avoids the open air. Whereas snakes and all creeping things love earth; all swimming things - love - water; winged things, air, of which they are the citizens; while those that fly still higher - love - the fire and have the habitat near it. Not that some of the animals as well do not love fire; for instance salamanders, for they even have their homes in it. It is because one or another of the elements doth form their bodies' outer envelope.

50. Each soul, accordingly, while it is in its body is weighted and constricted by these four.

Moreover it is natural it also should be pleased with some of them and pained with others.

For this cause, then, it doth not reach the height of its prosperity; still, as it is divine by nature, e'en while - wrapped up - in them, it struggles and it thinks, though not such thoughts as it would think were it set free from being bound in bodies.

Moreover if these - frames - are swept with storm and stress, or of disease or fear, then is the soul itself tossed on the waves, as man upon the deep with nothing steady under him.

CHAPTER VI

EGYPTIAN MAGIC

To the peoples of antiquity Egypt appeared as the very mother of magic. In the mysterious Nile country they found a magical system much more highly developed than any within their native knowledge, and the cult of the dead, with which Egyptian religion was so strongly identified, appeared to the foreigner to savour of magical practice. If the materials of the magical papyri be omitted, the accounts which we possess of Egyptian magic are almost wholly foreign, so that it is wiser to derive our data concerning it from the original native sources if we desire to arrive at a proper understanding of Egyptian sorcery.

Most of what has been written by Egyptologists on the subject of Egyptian magic has been penned on the assumption that magic is either merely a degraded form of religion, or its foundation. This is one of the results of the archæologist entering a domain - that of anthropology - where he is usually rather at a loss. For example, we find Sir Gaston Maspero stating that "ancient magic was the very foundation of religion. The faithful who desired to obtain some favor from a god had no chance of succeeding except by laying hands on the deity, and this arrest could only be effected by means of a certain number of rites, sacrifices, prayers, and chants, which the god himself had revealed and which obliged him to do what was demanded of him."[51] Then we find Dr. Budge stating that in the religious texts and works we see how magic is made to be the handmaiden of religion, and that whereas non-Egyptian races directed their art against the powers of darkness, and invoked a class of benevolent beings to their aid, the Egyptians aimed at complete control over their native deities.

Let us glance for a moment at the question of the origin of magic. Considerable diversity of opinion exists regarding this subject among present-day anthropologists, and the works of Frazer, Marett, Hubert, and Mauss, etc., although differing widely as regards its foundations, have thrown much light upon a hitherto obscure problem. All writers on the subject, however, appear to have ignored one notable circumstance in connection with it - that is, the element of wonder, which is the true fount and source of veritable magic. According to the warring schools of anthropology, nearly all magic is sympathetic or mimetic in its nature. For example, when the barbarian medicine-man desires rain he climbs a tree and sprinkles water upon the parched earth beneath, in the hope that the deity responsible for the weather will do likewise; when the ignorant sailor desires wind, he imitates the whistling of the gale. This system is universal, but if our conclusions are well founded, the magical element does not reside in such practices as these. It must be obvious, as Frazer has pointed out, that when the savage performs an act of sympathetic magic he does not regard it as magical - that is, to his way of thinking it does not contain any element of wonder at all; he regards his action as a cause which is certain to bring about the desired effect, exactly as the scientific man of today believes that if he follows certain formulæ certain results will be achieved. Now the true magic of wonder argues from effect to cause; so it would appear as if sympathy magic were merely a description of proto-science, due to mental processes entirely similar to those by which scientific laws are produced and scientific acts are performed - that there is a spirit of certainty about it which is not found, for example, in the magic of evocation.

It would, however, be rash to attempt to differentiate sympathetic magic entirely from what I would call the "magic of wonder" at this juncture; indeed, our knowledge of the basic laws of magic is too slight as yet to permit of such a process. We find considerable overlapping between the systems. For example, one of the ways by which evilly disposed persons could transform themselves into werewolves was by means of buckling on a belt of wolfskin. Thus we see that in this instance the true wonder-magic of animal transformation is in some measure connected with the sympathetic process, the idea being that the donning of wolfskin, or even the binding around one of a strip of the animal's hide, was sufficient to bestow the nature of the beast upon the wearer. In passing, I may say, for the sake of completeness, that I believe the magic of wonder to be almost entirely spiritistic in its nature, and that it consists of evocation and similar processes. Here, of course, it may be quoted against me that certain incenses, planetary signs, and other media known to possess affinities for certain supernatural beings were brought into use at the time of their evocation. Once more I admit that the two systems overlap; but that will not convince me that they are in essence the same.

ANTIQUITY OF EGYPTIAN MAGIC.

Like all magic, Egyptian magic was of prehistoric origin. As the savage of today employs the sympathetic process, so did the savage of the Egyptian Stone Age make use of it. That he also was fully aware of the spiritistic side of magic is certain. Animism is the mother of spiritism. The concept of the soul was arrived at at a comparatively early period in the history of man. The phenomenon of sleep puzzled him. Whither did the real man betake himself during the hours of slumber? The Palæolithic man watched his sleeping brother, who appeared to him as practically dead - dead, at least, to perception and the realities of life. Something seemed to have escaped the sleeper; the real, vital, and vivifying element had temporarily departed from him. From his own experience the puzzled savage knew that life did not cease with sleep, for in a more shadowy and unsubstantial sphere he re-enacted the scenes of his everyday existence. If the man during sleep had experiences in dreamland or in distant parts, it was only reasonable to suppose that his ego, his very self, had temporarily quitted the body. Grant so much, and you have two separate entities, body and soul, similar in appearance because the latter on the dream plane exercised functions identical with those of the former on the corporeal plane.

THE WANDERING SPIRIT.

But prehistoric logic did not stop here. So much premised, it extended its soul-theory to all animate beings, and even to things inanimate. Where, for example, did the souls of men go after death? Their bodies decayed, so it was only reasonable to suppose that they cast about them for other corporeal media. Failing their ability to enter the body of a new-born infant, they would take up their quarters in a tree, a rock, or any suitable natural object, and the terrified savage could hear their voices crying down the wind and whispering through the leaves of the forest, possibly clamoring or entreating for that food and shelter which they could not obtain in their disembodied condition. All nature, then, we see became animate to early man, and not less so to the early Egyptian than to others. But his hunting life had made prehistoric man exceptionally cunning and resourceful, and it would soon occur to him - in what manner we do not presume to say, as the point greatly requires elucidation - that we might possibly make use of such wandering and masterless spirits as he knew were close to his call. In this desire, it appears to me - if the statement be not a platitude - we have one of the origins of the magic of wonder, and certainly the origin of spiritism. Trading upon the wish of the disembodied spirit to materialize, prehistoric man would construct a fetish either in the human shape or in that of an animal, or in any weird presentment that squared with his ideas of spiritual existence. He usually made it of no great dimensions, as he did not believe that the alter ego, or soul, was of any great size. By threats or coaxings he prevailed upon the wandering spirit - whom he conceived as, like all the dead, cold, hungry, and homeless - to enter the little image, which duly became its corporeal abode, where its lips were piously smeared with the blood of animals slain in the chase, and where it was carefully attended. In return it was expected, by dint of its supernatural knowledge, that the soul contained in the fetish should assist its master or coadjutor in every possible way.

COERCING THE GODS.

Egyptian magic differed from most other systems in the circumstance that the native magician attempted to coerce certain of the gods into action on his behalf. Instances of this elsewhere are extremely rare, and it would seem as if the deities of Egypt had evolved in many cases from mere animistic conceptions. This is true in effect of all deities, but at a certain point in their history most gods arrive at such a condition of eminence that they soar far above any possibility of being employed by the magician as mere tools for any personal purpose. We often, however, find the broken-down, or deserted, deity coerced by the magician. Of this class Beelzebub might be taken as a good example. A great reputation is a hard thing to lose, and it is possible that the sorcerer may descry in the abandoned, and therefore idle, god a very suitable medium for this purpose. But we find the divinities of Egypt frightened into using their power on behalf of some paltry sorcerer even in the very zenith of their fame. One thing is of course essential to a complete system of sorcery, and that is the existence of a number of spirits, the detritus of a vanished or submerged religion. As we know, there were numerous strata in Egyptian religion - more than one faith had obtained on the banks of the Nile, and it may be that the worshippers of the deities of another as magical on the first introduction of a new system; in fact, these may have been interchangeable, and it is possible that by the time the various gods became common to all the practice had become so universal as to be impossible of abandonment.

If our conclusions are correct, it would seem that Maspero's statement that magic is the foundation of religion is scarcely consonant with fact. We have seen that at least the greater part of barbarian magic so - called - that is, sympathetic magic - is probably not of the nature of magic at all, so that the scope of his contention is considerably lessened. Budge's dictum that the magic of every other nation of the ancient East but the Egyptian was directed entirely against the powers of darkness, and was invented to frustrate their fell designs by invoking a class of benevolent beings, is so far an error in that the peoples of the ancient Orient invoked evil beings equally with good. At the same time it must be admitted that Egyptian magic had much more in common with religion than most other magical systems, and this arose from the extraordinary circumstances of the evolution of religion on Egyptian soil.

EGYPTIAN OCCULTISM AND SYMBOLISM

Of all civilizations known to us through history, that of ancient Egypt is the most marvellous, most fascinating, and most rich in occult significance: yet we have still much to discover, and although we have the assurance of Herodotus that the Egyptians were "beyond measure scrupulous in all matters appertaining to religion," the ancient religions - or such fragments as survive - appear at first glance confusing and even grotesque. It is necessary to remember that there was an inner as well as an outer theology, and that the occult mysteries were accessible only to those valiant and strenuous initiates who had successfully passed through a prolonged purification and course of preparation austere and difficult enough to discourage all save the most persistent and exalted spirits.

It is only available to us to wander on the outskirts of Egyptian mythology. The most familiar symbolic figures are those of Isis the moon goddess, traditional queen of Egypt, and Osiris her husband; and when we read that Isis was the sister, wife, and mother of Osiris we must seek the inner meaning of the strange and impossible relationship. It has been lucidly explained by Princess Karadja in her King Solomon: a Mystic Drama, 1912, pp. 130 to 131:

"Originally the dual souls are part of the same Divine Ego. They are golden fruits upon the great Tree of Life: 'male and female He created them.'

Isis is the Sister of Osiris because she is of Divine origin like himself, and is a sprit of equal rank.

She is his Wife, because she alone can fill his highest cravings.

She is his Mother because it is the mission of Woman to restore Man unto spiritual life."

How Osiris was slain by his brother Typhon - or Set - the spirit of evil, and dismembered into fourteen fragments which were scattered and bidden by the destroyer; how Isis, widowed and broken-hearted, sought patiently until she found each fragment, and how Horus her son when he grew to manhood challenged and conquered Typhon - all this is the figurative rendering of the eternal battle between light and darkness.

Typhon or Set symbolises autumn, decay, and destruction, Osiris springtime, light, and the fertilizing and growing powers of nature. Isis is typified in many forms, but was especially revered as the goddess of procreation, universal mother of the living, and protectress of the spirits of the dead.

Her symbol was the cow, and she is usually depicted wearing cow's horns, and between them the orb of the moon.

But more ancient and more exalted than Osiris was Ra, the sun god, whose worship was blended with that of Isis and her husband and son. The priests of Ra established a famous temple at Heliopolis, and founded a special system of solar worship. Just as the Emperor Constantine subsequently fixed as saints' days in the Christian church the days which had been dedicated to the ancient pagan gods, so the priests of Ra adapted their cult to the tastes and notions of the people, and a whole company of subordinate gods figured in the religions of lower Egypt for many centuries. Sometimes divine virtues were portrayed in very material forms.

Between 4000 and 2000 B.C., the worship of Amen, or Amen Ra, as the greatest god of the Egyptians, was established at Thebes, which became the centre of religious teaching. The priests grew more and more powerful until finally the high priest of Amen - whose name means the "hidden one" - became the king of upper Egypt. Amen was regarded as the creator, with all the power and attributes of Ra the sun god, and as ruler of the lesser gods.

It has been asked why the Egyptians, who had no belief in a material resurrection, took such infinite trouble to preserve the bodies of their dead. They looked forward to a paradise in which eternal life would be the reward of the righteous, and their creed inculcated faith in the existence of a spiritual body to be inhabited by the soul which had ended its earthly pilgrimage; but such beliefs do not explain the attention bestowed upon the lifeless corpse. The explanation must be sought in the famous Book of the Dead, representing the convictions which prevailed throughout the whole of the Egyptian civilization from pre-dynastic times. Briefly, the answer to our question is this: there was a Ka or double, in which the heart-soul was located; this Ka, equivalent to the astral body of modern occultists, was believed to be able to come into touch with material things through the preserved or mummified body. This theory accords with the axiom that each atom of physical substance has its relative equivalent on the astral plane. It will therefore be understood how, in the ancient religions, the image of a god was regarded as a medium through which his powers could be manifested.

"As above, so below"; every living thing possessed some divine attribute.

Faith in prayer was an essential article of the Egyptian religion, and the spoken word of a priest was believed to have strong potency, because it had been the words of Ra uttered by Thoth which brought the universe into being. Amulets inscribed with words were consequently thought to ensure the fulfilment of the blessing expressed, or the granting of the bliss desired.

The Book of the Dead was not only a guide to the life hereafter, wherein they would join their friends in the realms of eternal bliss, but gave detailed particulars of the necessary knowledge, actions, and, conduct during the earthly life to ensure a future existence in the spirit world, where everlasting life was the reward of the good and annihilation the fate of the wicked, thus showing that the belief in the existence of a future life was ever before them. Various qualities, though primarily considered a manifestation of the Almighty, were attributed each to a special god who controlled and typified one particular virtue. This partly accounts for the multiplied numbers of the Egyptian gods, and with the further complications that resulted from invasions and the adoption of alien beliefs, the religious philosophy of Egypt is not easy to follow, and is often seemingly contradictory; but when we take into consideration the vast period during which this empire flourished it is natural that the external manifestations of faith should have varied as time went on.

A knowledge of life, death, and resurrection of Osiris is assumed, and his worship in association with Isis and Horus although not necessarily under these names, is continuous. Horus is frequently alluded to as the god of the ladder, and the mystic ladder seen by Jacob in his vision, and the ladder of seven steps known to the initiates of Egypt, Greece, Mexico, India, and Persia will be familiar to all students of occultism.

Throughout the whole of the Egyptian civilization, which lasted for at least 6000 years, the influence and potency of amulets and talismans was recognised in the religious services, each talisman and amulet having a specified virtue.

Certain amulets not only were worn during life, but were even attached to the dead body. They are described in the following notes

The Crux Ansata, or Ankh (see Illustrations Nos. 1, 2, 3, Plate I), was known as the symbol of life, the loop at the top of the cross consisting of the hieroglyphic

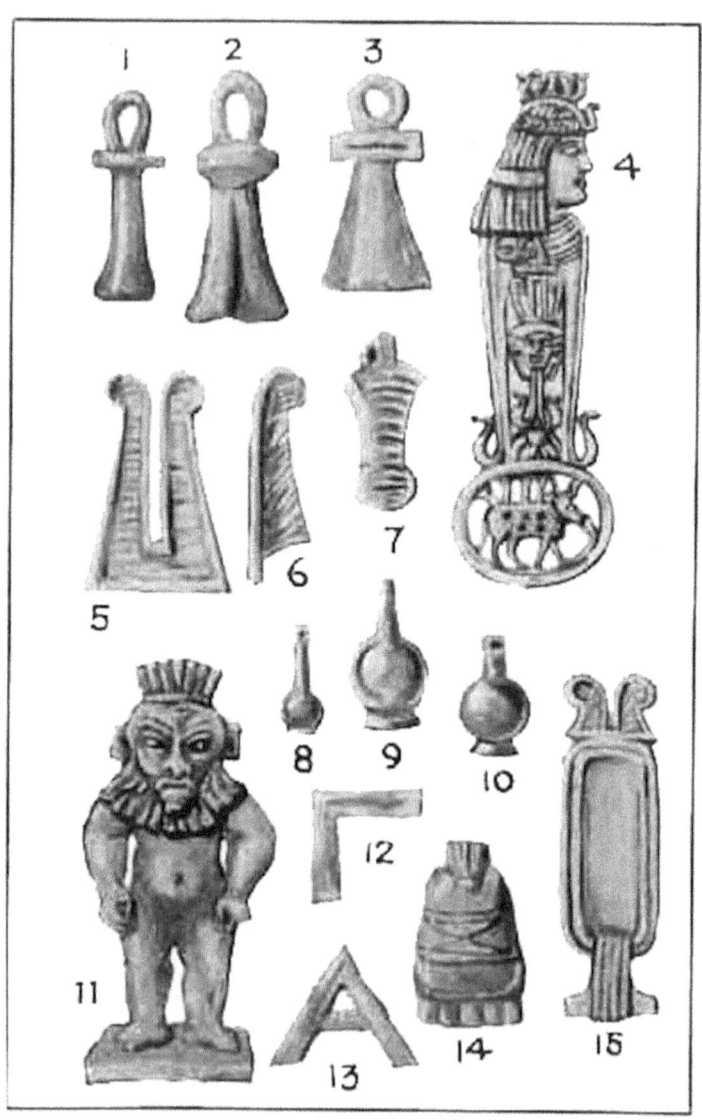

Plate I: EGYPTIAN TALISMANS

Ru (O) set in an upright form, meaning the gateway, or mouth, the creative power being signified by the loop which represents a fish's mouth giving birth to water as the life of the country, bringing the inundations and renewal of the fruitfulness of the earth to those who depended upon its increase to maintain life. It was regarded as the key of the Nile which overflowed periodically and so fertilized the land.

It was also shown in the hands of the Egyptian kings, at whose coronations it played an important part, and the gods are invariably depicted holding this symbol of creative power; it was also worn to bring knowledge, power, and abundance. Again, it had reference to the spiritual life for it was from the Crux Ansata, or Ankh, that the symbol of Venus originated, the circle over the cross being the triumph of spirit, represented by the circle, over matter, shown by the cross.

The Menat (Illustrations Nos. 4, 7, Plate I), were specially dedicated to Hathor, who was a type of Isis, and was worn for conjugal happiness, as it gave power and strength to the organs of reproduction, promoting health and fruitfulness. It frequently formed a part of a necklace, and was elaborately ornamented; No, 4 from the British Museum, is a good specimen, the cow being an emblem of the maternal qualities which were the attributes of the goddess, who stood for all that is good and true in wife, mother, and daughter.

The Two Plumes (Illustration No. 5, Plate I), are sun amulets and the symbols of Ra and Thoth, the two feathers being typical of the two lives, spiritual and material. This was worn to promote uprightness in dealing, enlightenment, and morality, being symbolical of the great gods of light and air.

The Single Plume (Illustration No. 6, Plate I), was an emblem of Maat, the female counterpart of Thoth, who wears on her head the feather characteristic of the phonetic value of her name; she was the personification of integrity, righteousness, and truth.

Illustrations Nos. 8, 9, 10, Plate I, show three forms of the Nefer, a symbol of good luck, worn to attract success, happiness, vitality, and friends.

The Cartouche, or Name Amulet (Illustration No. 15, Plate I), was worn to secure favor, recognition, and remembrance, and to prevent the name of its wearer being blotted out in the next world. This is a very important amulet, as the name was believed to be an integral part of the man, without which his soul could not come before God, so that it was most essential that the name should be preserved, in order, as described in the Book of the Dead, "thou shalt never perish, thou shalt never, never come to an end," the loss of the name meaning the total annihilation of the individual.

The amulets of the Angles (see Illustrations Nos. 12, 13, Plate I) and the Plummet (No. 60 on the same Plate), were symbols of the god Thoth, and were worn for moral integrity, wisdom, knowledge, order, and truth. Thoth was the personification of law and order, being the god who worked out the creation as decreed by the god Ra. He knew all the words of power and the secrets of all hearts, and may be regarded as the chief recording angel; he was also the inventor of all arts and sciences.

Bes, shown in Illustration No. 11, Plate I, was a very popular talisman, being the god of laughter, merry-making, and good luck; by some authorities he is considered to be a foreign importation from pre-dynastic times, and he has been identified with Horus and regarded as the god who renewed youth. He was also the patron of beauty, the protector of children, and was undoubtedly the progenitor of the modern Billiken.

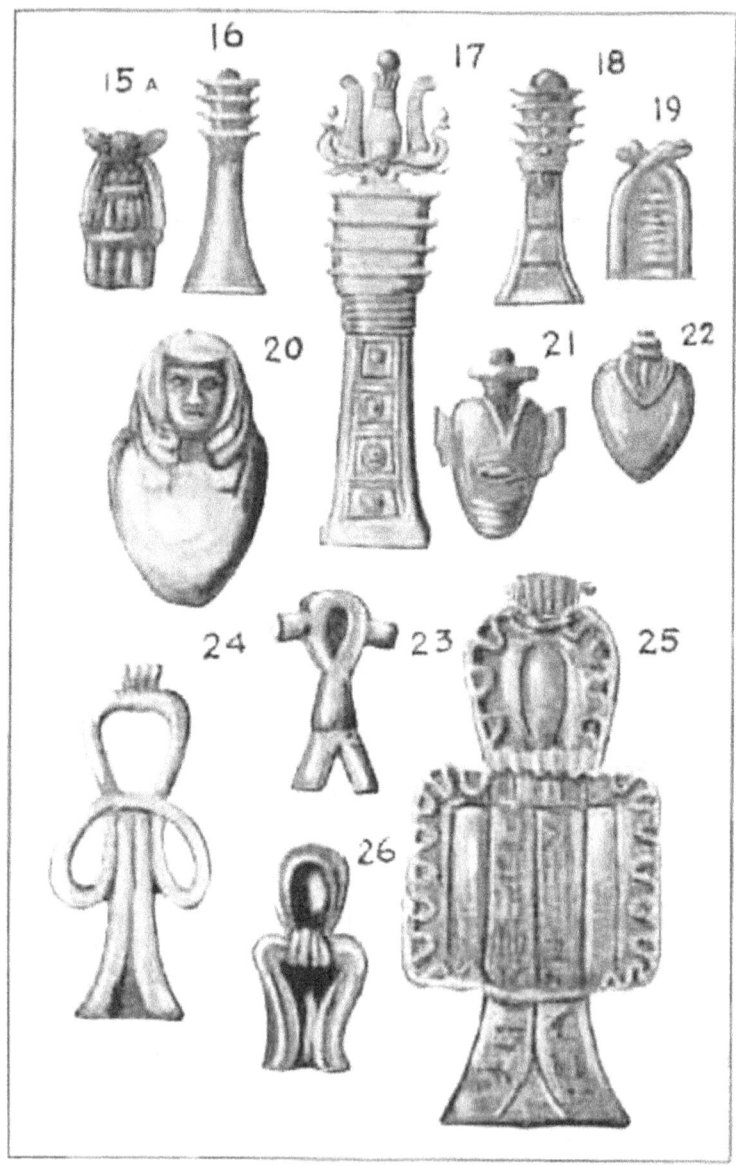

PLATE II. EGYPTIAN TALISMANS

Illustrations Nos. 15, 19, Plate II, are examples of the Aper, which symbolised providence and was worn for steadfastness, stability, and alertness.

The Tat (Illustrations Nos. 16, 17, 18, Plate II) held a very important place in the religious services of the Egyptians, and formed the centre of the annual ceremony of the setting-up of the Tat, a service held to commemorate the death and resurrection of Osiris, this symbol representing the building-up of the backbone and reconstruction of the body of Osiris. In their services the Egyptians associated themselves with Osiris, through whose sufferings and death they hoped to rise glorified and immortal, and secure everlasting happiness. The four cross-bars symbolise the four cardinal points, and the four elements of earth, air, fire and water, and were often very elaborately ornamented (see Illustration No. 17, Plate II, taken from an example at the British Museum). It was worn as a talisman for stability and strength, and for protection from enemies; also that all doors - or opportunities - might be open both in this life and the next. Moreover, a Tat of gold set in sycamore wood, which had been steeped in the water of Ankham flowers, was placed at the neck of the deceased on the day of interment, to protect him on his journey through the underworld and assist him in triumphing over his foes, that he might become perfect for ever and ever.

The Heart was believed to be the seat of the soul, and Illustrations Nos. 20, 21, 22, Plate II, are examples of these talismans worn to prevent black magicians from bewitching the soul out of the body. The importance of these charms will be realized from the belief that if the soul left the heart, the body would quickly fade away and die. According to Egyptian lore at the judgment of the dead the heart is weighed, when, if found perfect, it is returned to its owner, who immediately recovers his powers of locomotion and becomes his own master, with strength in his limbs and everlasting felicity in his soul.

The buckle of the girdle of Isis was worn to obtain the good-will and protection of this goddess, and symbolised "the blood of Isis" and her strength and power. Frequently made of carnelian it was believed to protect its wearer from every kind of evil; also to secure the good-will of Horus; and, when placed like the golden Tat at the neck of the dead on the day of the funeral in the soul's journey through the underworld it opened up all hidden places and procured the favor of Isis and her son,

Horus, for ever and ever. (See Illustrations Nos. 24, 25, 26, Plate II.)

The Tie, or Sa (No.23, Plate II) is the symbol of Ta-urt, the hippopotamus-headed goddess, who was associated with the Thoth, the personification of divine intelligence and human reason; it was worn for magical protection.

The Scarab was the symbol of Khepera, a form of the sun-god who transforms inert matter into action, creates life, and typifies the glorified spiritual body that man shall possess at the resurrection. From the enormous number of scarabs that have been found, this must have formed the most popular of the talismans. The symbol was derived from a beetle, common in Egypt, which deposits its eggs in a ball of clay, the action of the insect in rolling this ball along the ground being compared with the sun itself in its progress across the sky; and as the ball contained the living germ which (under the heat of the sun) hatched out into a beetle, so the scarab became the symbol of creation. It is also frequently seen holding the disk of the sun between its claws, with wings extended, and it is thought by some authorities that the scarab was taken as an emblem of the sun, because the burial of its ball was symbolic of the setting sun from which new life arises with each dawn.

Scarabs of green stones with rims of gold were buried in the heart of the deceased, or laid upon the breast, with a written prayer for his protection on the day of judgment, whilst words of power were frequently recited over the scarab which was placed under the coffin as an emblem of immortality so that no fiend could harm the dead in his journey through the underworld. It is said the scarab was associated with burial as far back as the fourth dynasty (about 4600 B.C.); it represented matter about to pass from a state of inertness into active life, so was considered a fitting emblem of resurrection and immortality, typifying not only the sun's disk, but the evolutions of the soul throughout eternity. It was also worn by the Egyptian warriors in their signet rings for health, strength, and virility, it being thought that this species of beetle was all males, so that it would attract all. manly qualities, both of mind and body. For this reason it was very popular as presents between friends, many scarabs being found with good wishes or mottoes engraved on the under side, and some of the kings used the back of scarabs to commemorate historical events; one in the British Museum records the slaughter of one hundred and two fierce lions by Amenhetep III, with his own hand (see Illustrations Nos. 27, 28, Plate III).

Next to the scarab, the ancient Egyptians attached much importance to the Eye Amulet, which, from the earliest astral mythology, was first represented by the point within the circle and was associated with the god of the pole star, which, from its fixity, was taken as a type of the eternal, unchangeable as time rolled on, and thus a fitting emblem of fixity of purpose, poise, and stability. Later it was one of the hieroglyphic signs of the sun-god Ra, and represented the one supreme power casting his eye over all the world, and instead of the point within the circle is sometimes represented as a widely open eye. This symbol was also assigned to Osiris, Isis, Horus, and Ptah; the amulet known as the Eye of Osiris being placed upon the incision made in the side of the body - for the purpose of embalming - to watch over and guard the soul of the deceased during its passing through the darkness of the tomb to the life beyond.

It was also worn by the living to ensure health and protection from the blighting influence of workers in black magic, and for the stability, strength, and courage of Horus, the wisdom and understanding of Ptah, and the foresight of Isis.

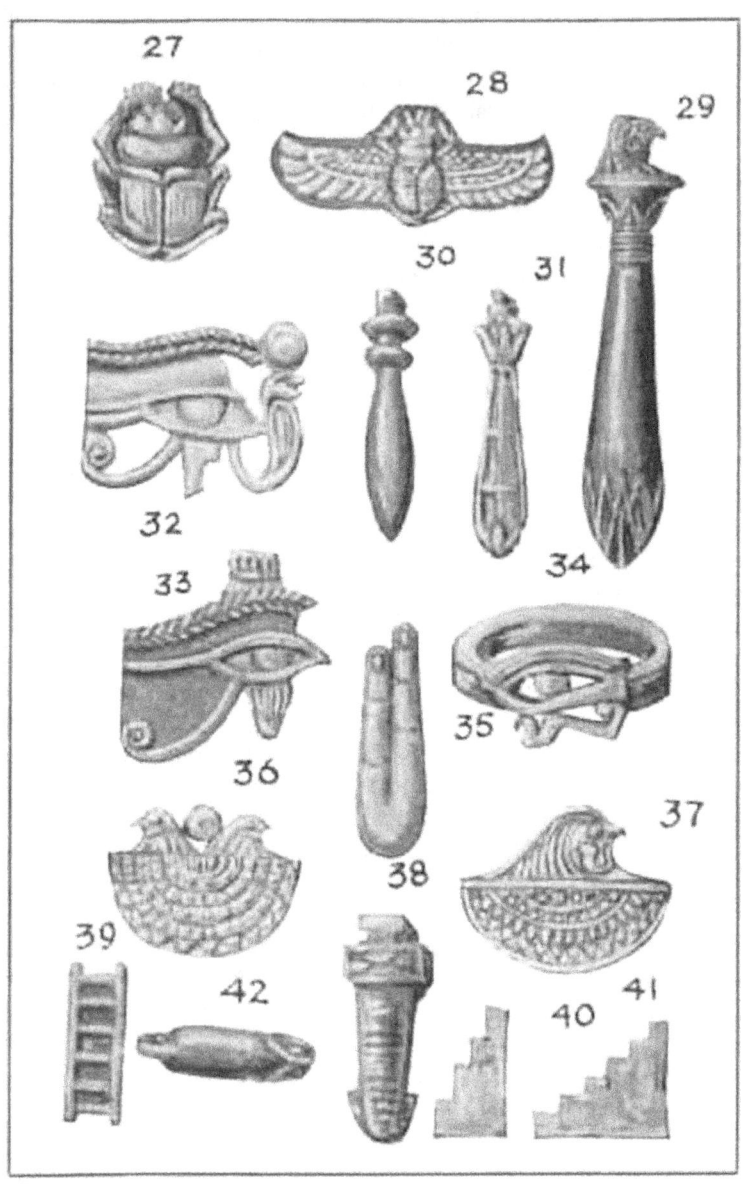

PLATE III. EGYPTIAN TALISMANS

It was also extensively used in necklaces on account of the idea that representations of the eye itself would watch over and guard its wearer from the malignant glances of the envious, it being universally believed that the fiery sparks of jealousy, hatred, and malice darting from the eyes of angry persons, envious of the good looks, health, and success of the fortunate ones, could so poison the surrounding atmosphere as even to cause sickness, decay, and death; horses were thought particularly liable to this injurious influence, and talismans to avert such a misfortune to them were hung on their foreheads, or over the left eye.

Examples of eye amulets are illustrated on Plate III, Nos. 32, 33, and 34.

When two eyes are used together the right eye is symbolic of Ra, or Osiris and the sun; whilst the left eye represents Isis, or the moon, and is sometimes called the amulet of the two Utchats; the word Utchat, signifying "strength," being applied to the sun when he enters the summer solstice about June 22d, his strength and power on earth being greatest at that time.

The talisman of the Two Fingers (Illustration No. 35, Plate III) was symbolical of help, assistance, and benediction, typified by the two fingers extended by Horus to assist his father in mounting the ladder suspended between this world and the next. This amulet was frequently placed in the interior of the mummified body to enable the departed to travel quickly to the regions of the blest. Amongst the ancient Egyptians the fingers were ever considered an emblem of strength and power, the raising of the first two fingers being regarded as a sign of peace and good faith; the first finger being the indicator of divine will and justice and the only one that can stand erect by itself alone; the second representing the holy spirit, the mediator, a symbolism handed down to us in the extension of the index and medius in the ecclesiastical benediction. It is also interesting to note that at the marriage ceremony in olden days the ring was first placed on the thumb, as typical of man's allegiance to God, and lastly on the third finger of his bride to show that next to God in the trinity, a man's life should be devoted to his wife.

The Collar Amulet (Illustrations Nos. 36, 37, Plate III) was a symbol of Isis, and was worn to procure her protection and the strength of her son Horus. In both examples the head of the hawk appears, this bird being attributed to Horus as well as to Ra. This collar, which was made of gold, was engraved with words of power and seems to have been chiefly used as a funeral amulet.

The Sma (Illustration No. 38, Plate III) was a favorite amulet from the dawn of Egyptian history, and is frequently used in various forms of decorated art. It was symbolical of union and stability of affection, and was worn to strengthen love and friendship and ensure physical happiness and faithfulness.

The Ladder is a symbol of Horus, and was worn to secure his assistance in overcoming and surmounting difficulties in the material world, as well as to form a connection with the heaven world, or land of light. The earliest traditions place this heaven world above the earth, its floor being the sky, and to reach this a ladder was deemed necessary. From the pyramid texts it seems there were two stages of ascent to the upper paradise, represented by two ladders, one being the ladder of Sut, forming the ladder of ascent from the land of darkness, and the other the ladder of Horus reaching the land of light (Illustration No. 39, Plate III).

'The Steps (Illustrations Nos. 40, 41, Plate III) are a symbol of Osiris, who is described as the god of the staircase, through whom it was hoped the deceased might reach the heaven world and attain everlasting bliss.

The Snake's Head talisman (Illustration No. 42, Plate III) was worn to protect its wearer from the attacks of Rerek, or Apep, the servant of Set, who was typified as a terrible serpent, which when killed had the power of rising in new forms and who obstructed the passage to the heaven world. The serpent, although sometimes assumed to be a form of evil, was generally regarded as a protecting influence, and for this reason was usually sculptured on either side of the doorways to the tombs of kings, temples, and other sacred buildings to guard the dead from enemies of every kind, and to prevent the entrance of evil in any shape or form. It was also placed round the heads of divinities and round the crowns of their kings as a symbol of royal might and power, being one of the forms or types of Tem the son of Ptah, who is thought by some authorities to have been the first living man god of the Egyptians, and the god of the setting sun (in contrast to Horus, who was the god of the rising sun). Tem was typified by a huge snake, and it is curious to note in connection with this that amongst country folk at the present day there is a popular belief that a serpent will not die until the sun goes down.

The Sun's Disk talismans (Illustrations No. 43, 45, Plate IV) are symbols of the god Ra, No. 45 being appropriately placed upon the head of a ram, the symbol of the zodiacal house Aries, in which sign the sun is exalted. It was worn for power and renown, and to obtain the favors of the great ones, being also an emblem of new birth and resurrection.

The Frog talisman (Illustration No. 44, Plate IV) was highly esteemed, and is an attribute of Isis, being worn to attract her favors and for fruitfulness. Because of its fertility its hieroglyphic meaning was an immense number. It was also used as a symbol of Ptah, as it represented life in embryo, and by the growth of its feet after birth it typified strength from weakness, and was worn for recovery from disease, also for health and long life, taking the place sometimes of the Crux Ansata or Ankh, as a symbol of life.

The Pillow (Illustration No. 46, Plate IV) was used for preservation from sickness and against pain and suffering; it was also worn for the favor of Horns, and was placed with the dead as a protection and to prevent violation of the tomb.

The Lotus (Illustrations No. 47, 48, Plate IV) is a symbol with two meanings. Emblematical of the sun in the ancient days of Egypt and typifying light, understanding, fruitfulness, and plenty, it was believed to bring the favors of the god Ra. Later it is described as "the pure lily of the celestial ocean," the symbol of Isis, who is sometimes alluded to as "the white virgin." It became typical of virginity and purity, and having the double virtue of chastity and fecundity it was alike prized for maiden- and motherhood.

The Fish talisman (Illustrations Nos. 49, 50, Plate IV) is a symbol of Hathor

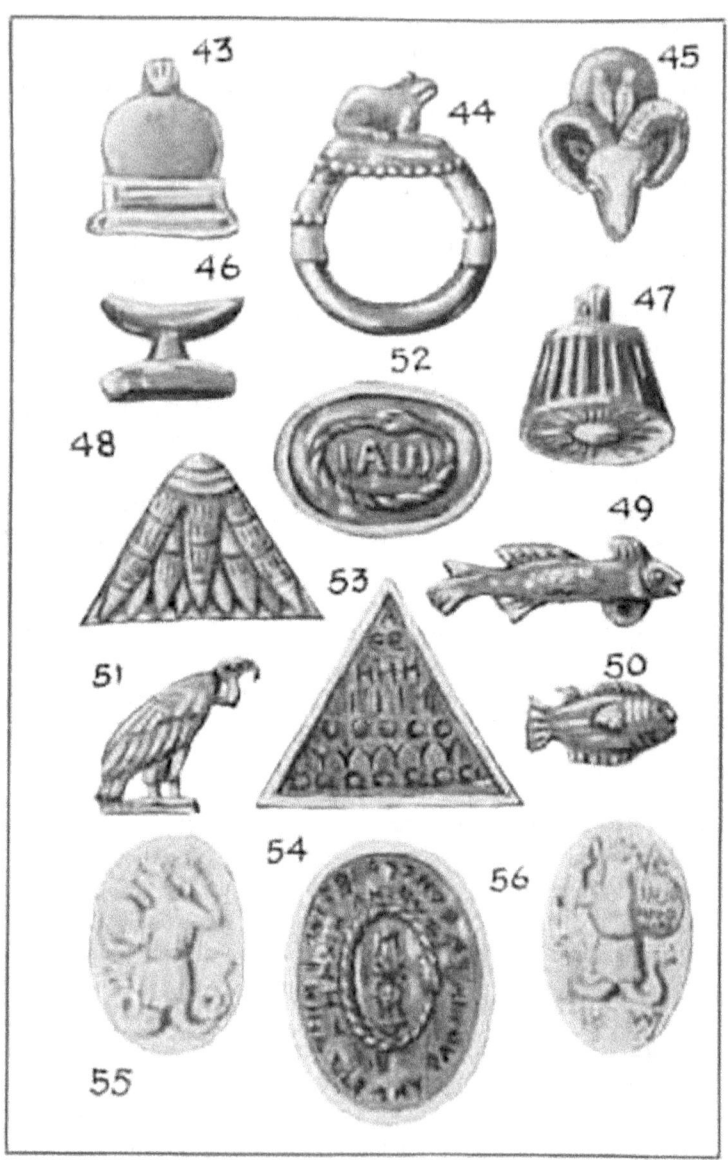

PLATE IV. EGYPTIAN TALISMANS

- who controlled the rising of the Nile - as well as an amulet under the influence of Isis and Horus. It typified the primeval creative principle and was worn for domestic felicity, abundance, and general prosperity.

The Vulture talisman (Illustration No. 51, Plate IV) was worn to protect from the bites of scorpions, and to attract motherly love and protection of Isis, who, it was believed, assumed the form of a vulture when searching for her son Horus, who, in her absence, had been stung to death by a scorpion. Thoth, moved by her lamentations, came to earth and gave her "the words of power," which enabled her to restore Horus to life. For this reason, it was thought that this amulet would endow its wearer with power and wisdom so that he might identify himself with Horus and partake of his good fortune in the fields of eternal bliss.

It is, of course, difficult and futile to speculate as to the extent of the influence these Egyptian amulets and talismans exercised over this ancient people, but in the light of our present knowledge we feel that the religious symbolism they represented, the conditions under which they were made, the faith in their efficacy, and the invocations and "words of power" which in every case were a most essential part of their mysterious composition makes them by far the most interesting of any yet dealt with.

Gnosticism is the name given to a system of religion which came into existence in the Roman empire about the time Christianity was established; it was founded on a philosophy known in Asia Minor centuries previously and apparently based upon the Egyptian beliefs, the Zendavesta, Buddhism, and the Kabala, with their conception of the perpetual conflict between good and evil.

The name is derived from the Greek Gnosis, meaning knowledge, and, in brief, the gnostics' belief was that the intellectual world, with its spirits, intelligences, and various orders of angels were created by the Almighty, and that the visible matter of creation was an emanation from these powers and forces.

The attributes of the Supreme Being were those of Kabala: - Wisdom - Jeh; prudence - Jehovah; magnificence - El; severity - Elohim; victory and glory - Zaboath; empire - Adonai; the Gnostics also took from the Talmud the planetary princes and the angels under them.

Basilides, the Gnostic priest, taught that God first created

(1) Nous, or mind; from this emanated

(2) Logos, the Word; from this

(3) Phronesis, Intelligence; and from this

(4) Sophia, Wisdom; and from the last

(5) Dynamis, Strength.

The Almighty was known as Abraxas, which signifies in Coptic "the Blessed Name," and was symbolized by a figure, the head of which is that of a cock, the body that of a man, with serpents forming the legs; in his right hand he holds a whip, and on his left arm is a shield. This talisman (see Illustrations Nos. 55, 56, Plate IV) is a combination of the five emanations mentioned above: Nous and Logos are expressed by the two serpents, symbols of the inner sense and understanding, the bead of the cock representing Phronesis, for foresight and vigilance; the two arms hold the symbols of Sophia and Dynamis, the shield of wisdom and the whip of power, worn for protection from moral and physical ill.

The Gnostics had great faith in the efficacy of sacred names and sigils when engraved on stones as talismans; also in magical symbols derived principally from the Kabala.

One of the most popular inscriptions was Iaw (Jehovah), and in Illustration No. 52, Plate IV, this is shown surrounded by the serpent Khnoubis, taken from the Egyptian philosophy, representing the creative principles, and was worn for vitality, understanding, and protection. The seven Greek vowels (Illustration No. 53, Plate IV) symbolized the seven heavens, or planets, whose harmony keeps the universe in existence, each vowel having seven different methods of expression corresponding with a certain force, the correct utterance of these letters and comprehension of the forces typified being believed to confer supreme power, bringing success in all enterprises and giving complete control over all the powers of darkness.

Illustration No. 54, Plate IV, is an example of the use of the magic symbols, the meaning of which has been lost. It is probably a composition of the initial letters of some mystical sigil, enclosed by a serpent and the names of the arch-angels Gabriel, Paniel, Ragauel, Thureiel, Souriel, and Michael. It was worn for health and success; also for protection from all evils, and it is cut in an agate and set in a gold mount.

A figure of a serpent with a lion's head, usually surrounded with a halo, was worn to protect its wearer from heart and chest complaints and to drive away demons.

The mystic Aum, already described in the chapter on Indian talismans, was also a favorite with the Gnostics, and equally popular was a talisman composed of the vowels I A Ω, repeated to make twelve, this number representing the ineffable name of God, which, according to the Talmud, was only communicated to the most pious of the priesthood. They also adopted from the Egyptians the following symbols: Horus, usually represented seated on a Lotus, for fertility; Osiris, usually in the form of a mummified figure, for spiritual attainment; and Isis for the qualities mentioned in the previous chapter.

Footnotes
51. "Etudes de Mythologie et d'Archéologie Egyptienne;" Paris, 1893.

CHAPTER VII

THE VISION OF HERMES[52]

One day, Hermes, after reflecting on the origin of things, fell asleep. A dull torpor took possession of his body; but in proportion as the latter grew benumbed, his spirit ascended into space. Then an immense being, of indeterminate form, seemed to call him by name.

"Who art thou?" said the terrified Hermes.

"I am Osiris, the sovereign Intelligence who is able to unveil all things. What desirest thou?"

"To behold the source of beings, O divine Osiris, and to know God."

"Thou shalt be satisfied."

Immediately Hermes felt himself plunged in a delicious light. In its pellucid billows passed the ravishing forms of all beings. Suddenly, a terrifying encircling darkness descended upon him.

Hermes was in a humid chaos, filled with smoke and with a heavy, rumbling sound. Then a voice rose from the abyss, the cry of light. At once a quick-leaping flame darted forth from the humid depths, reaching to the ethereal heights. Hermes ascended with it, and found himself again in the expanse of space. Order began to clear up chaos in the abyss; choruses of constellations spread above his head and the voice of light filled infinity.

"Dost thou understand what thou hast seen?" said Osiris to Hermes, bound down in his dream and suspended between earth and sky.

"No," said Hermes.

"Thou wilt now learn. Thou hast just seen what exists from all eternity. The light thou didst first see is the divine intelligence which contains all things in potentiality, enclosing the models of all beings. The darkness in which thou wast afterwards plunged is the material world on which the men of earth live. But the fire thou didst behold shooting forth from the depths, is the divine Word. God is the Father, the Word is the son, and their union is Life."

"What marvellous sense has opened out to me?" asked Hermes. "I no longer see with the eyes of the body, but with those of the spirit. How has that come to pass?"

"Child of dust," replied Osiris, "it is because the Word is in thee. That in thee which hears, sees, and acts is the Word itself, the sacred fire, the creative utterance!"

"Since things are so," said Hermes, "grant that I may see the light of the worlds; the path of souls from which man comes and to which he returns."

"Be it done according to thy desire."

Hermes became heavier than a stone and fell through space like a meteorite. Finally he reached the summit of a mountain. It was night, the earth was gloomy and deserted, and his limbs seemed as heavy as iron.

"Raise thine eyes and look!" said the voice of Osiris.

Then Hermes saw a wonderful sight. The starry heavens, stretching through infinite space, enveloped him with seven luminous spheres. In one glance, Hermes saw the seven heavens stretching above his head, tier upon tier, like seven transparent and concentric globes, the sidereal centre of which he now occupied. The milky way formed the girdle of the last. In each sphere there rolled a planet accompanied by a genius of different form, sign and light. Whilst Hermes, dazzled by the sight, was contemplating their wide-spread efflorescence and majestic movements, the voice said to him:

"Look, listen, and understand. Thou seest the seven spheres of all life. Through them is accomplished the fall and ascent of souls. The seven genii are the seven rays of the word-light. Each of them commands one sphere of the spirit, one phase of the life of souls. The one nearest to thee is the Genius of the Moon, with his disquieting smile and crown of silver sickle. He presides over births and deaths, sets free souls from bodies and draws them into his ray. Above him, pale Mercury points out the path to ascending or descending souls with his caduceus, which contains all knowledge. Higher still, shining Venus holds the mirror of love, in which souls forget and recognize them in turn. Above her, the Genius of the Sun raises the triumphal torch of eternal beauty. At a yet loftier height, Mars brandishes the sword of justice. Enthroned on the azure sphere, Jupiter holds the sceptre of supreme power, which is divine intelligence. At the boundaries of the world, beneath the signs of the Zodiac, Saturn bears the globe of universal wisdom.[53]

"I see," said Hermes, "the seven regions which comprise the visible and invisible world; I see the seven rays of the word-light, of the one God who traverses them and governs them by these rays. Still, O master, how does mankind journey through all these worlds?"

"Dost thou see," said Osiris, "a luminous seed fall from the regions of the milky way into the seventh sphere? These are germs of souls. They live like faint vapors in the region of Saturn, gay and free from care, knowing not their own happiness. On falling from sphere to sphere, however, they put on increasingly heavier envelopes. In each incarnation they acquire a new corporeal sense, in harmony with the surroundings in which they are living. Their vital energy increases, but in proportion as they enter into denser bodies they lose the memory of their celestial origin. Thus is effected the fall of souls which come from the divine ether. Ever more and more captivated by matter and intoxicated by life, they fling themselves like a rain of fire, with quiverings of voluptuous delight, through the regions of grief, love, and death, right into their earthly prison where thou thyself lamentest, held down by the fiery centre of the earth, and where divine life appears to thee nothing more than an empty dream."

"Can souls die?" asked Hermes.

"Yes," replied the voice of Osiris, "many perish in the fatal descent. The soul is the daughter of heaven, and its journey is a test. If it loses the memory of its origin, in its unbridled love of matter, the divine spark which was in it and which might have become more brilliant than a star, returns to the ethereal region, a lifeless atom, and the soul disaggregates in the vortex of gross elements."

Hermes shuddered at these words, for a raging tempest enveloped him in a black mist. The seven spheres disappeared beneath dense vapors. In them he saw human spectres uttering strange cries, carried off and torn by phantoms of monsters and animals, amidst nameless groans and blasphemies.

"Such is the destiny," said Osiris, "of souls irremediably base and evil. Their torture finishes only with their destruction, which includes the loss of all consciousness. The vapors are now dispersing, the seven spheres reappear beneath the firmament. Look on this side. Do you see this swarm of souls trying to mount once more to the lunar regions? Some are beaten back to earth like eddies of birds beneath the might of the tempest. The rest with mighty wings reach the upper sphere, which draws them with it as it rotates. Once they have come to this sphere, they recover their vision of divine things. This time, however, they are not content to reflect them in the dream of a powerless happiness; they become impregnated thereby with the lucidity of a grief-enlightened consciousness, the energy of a will acquired through struggle and strife. They become luminous, for they possess the divine in themselves and radiate it in their acts. Strengthen therefore thy soul, O Hermes! calm thy darkened mind by contemplating these distant flights of souls which mount the seven spheres and are scattered about therein like sheaves of sparks. Thou also canst follow them, but a strong will it needs to rise. Look how they swarm and form into divine choruses. Each places itself beneath its favorite genius. The most beautiful dwell in the solar region; the most powerful rise to Saturn. Some ascend to the Father, powers themselves amidst powers. For where everything ends, everything eternally begins; and the seven spheres say together: 'Wisdom! Love! Justice! Beauty! Splendor! Knowledge! Immortality!'"

"This," said the hierophant, "is what ancient Hermes saw and what his successors have handed down to us. The words of the wise are like the seven notes of the lyre which contains all music, along with the numbers and the laws of the universe, The vision of Hermes resembles the starry heaven, whose unfathomable depths are strewn with constellations. For the child this is nothing more than a gold-studded vault, for the sage it is boundless space in which worlds revolve, with their wonderful rhythms and cadences. The vision contains the eternal numbers, evoking signs and magic keys. The more thou learnest to contemplate and understand it, the farther thou shalt see its limits extend, for the same organic law governs all worlds."

The prophet of the temple commented on the sacred text. He explained that the doctrine of the word-light represents divinity in the static condition, in its perfect balance. He showed its triple nature, which is at once intelligence, force, and matter; spirit, soul, and body; light, word, and life. Essence, manifestation, and substance are three terms which take each other for granted. Their union constitutes the divine and intellectual principle par excellence, the law of the ternary unity which governs creation from above downwards.

Having thus led his disciple to the ideal centre of the universe, the generating principle of Being, the master spread him abroad in time and space in a multiple efflorescence. For a second part of the vision represents divinity in the dynamic condition, i.e., in active evolution; in other terms, the visible and invisible universe, the living heavens. The seven spheres attached to the seven planets symbolise seven principles, seven different states of matter and spirit, seven different worlds which each man and each humanity are forced to pass through in their evolution across a solar system. The seven genii or the seven cosmogonic gods signify the superior, directing spirits of all spheres, the offspring themselves of inevitable evolution. To an initiate of old, therefore, each great god was the symbol and patron of legions of spirits which reproduced his type in a thousand varieties, and which, from their own sphere, could exercise their action over mankind and terrestrial things. The seven genii of the vision of Hermes are the seven Devas of India, the seven Amshapands of Persia, the seven great Angels of Chaldæa, the seven Sephiroths of the Kabbala, the seven Archangels of the Christian Apocalypse. The great septenary which enfolds the universe does not vibrate in the seven colors of the rainbow and the seven notes of the scale, only; it also manifests itself in the constitution of man, which is triple in essence, but sevenfold in its evolution.

"Thus," said the hierophant in conclusion, "thou hast reached the very threshold of the great arcanum. The divine life has appeared to thee beneath the phantoms of reality. Hermes has unfolded to thee the invisible heavens, the light of Osiris, the hidden God of the universe who breathes in millions of souls and animates thereby the wandering globes and working bodies. It is now thine to direct thy path and choose the road leading to the pure spirit. Henceforth dost thou belong to those who have been brought back from death to life. REMEMBER THAT THERE ARE TWO MAIN KEYS TO KNOWLEDGE. This is the first: 'The without is like the within of things; the small is like the large; there is only one law and he who works is One. In the divine economy, there is nothing either great or small.' And this is the second: 'Men are mortal gods and gods are immortal men.' Happy the man who understands these words, for he holds the key to all things. Remember that the law of mystery veils the great truth. Total knowledge can be revealed only to our brethren who have gone through the same trials as ourselves. Truth must be measured according to intelligence; it must be veiled from the feeble, whom it would madden, and concealed from the wicked, who are capable of seizing only its fragments, which they would turn into weapons of destruction. Keep it in thy heart and let it speak through thy work. Knowledge will be thy might, faith thy sword, and silence thy armor that cannot be broken."

The revelations of the prophet of Amon-Râ, which opened out to the new initiate such vast horizons over himself and over the universe, doubtless produced a profound impression, when uttered from the observatory of a Theban temple, in the clear calm of an Egyptian night. The pylons, the white roofs, and terraces of the temples lay asleep at his feet between the dark clusters of nopals and tamarind trees. Away in the distance were large monolithic shrines, colossal statues of the gods, seated like incorruptible judges on their silent lake. Three pyramids, geometrical figures of the tetragram and of the sacred septenary, could be dimly seen on the horizon, their triangles clearly outlined in the light grey air. The unfathomable firmament was studded with stars. With what a strange gaze he looked at those constellations which were depicted to him as future dwellings! When finally the gold-tipped barque of the moon rose above the dark mirror of the Nile which died away on the horizon, like a long bluish serpent, the neophyte believed he saw the barque of Isis floating over the river of souls which it carries off towards the sun of Osiris. He remembered the Book of the Dead, and the meaning of all the symbols was now unveiled to his mind after what he had seen and learned; he might believe himself to be in the crepuscular kingdom of the Amenti, the mysterious interregnum between the earthly and the heavenly life, where the departed, who are at first without eyes and power of utterance, by degrees regain sight and voice. He, too, was about to undertake the great journey, the journey of the infinite, through worlds and existences. Hermes had already absolved him and judged him to be worthy. He had given him the explanation of the great enigma "One only soul, the great soul of the All, by dividing itself out, has given birth to all the souls that struggle throughout the universe." Armed with the mighty secret, he entered the barque of Isis. Rising aloft into the ether, it floated in the interstellar regions. The broad rays of a far-spreading dawn were already piercing the azure veils of the celestial horizons, and the choir of the glorious spirits, the Akhimou-Sekou, who have attained to eternal repose, was chanting: "Rise, Râ Hermakouti, sun of spirits! Those in thy barque are in exaltation. They raise exclamations in the barque of millions of years. The great divine cycle overflows with joy when glorifying the mighty sacred barque. Rejoicing is taking place in the mysterious chapel. Rise, Ammon-Râ Hermakouti, thou self-creating sun!" And the initiate replied proudly: "I have attained the country of truth and justification. I rise from the dead as a living god, and shine forth in the choir of the gods who dwell in heaven, for I belong to their race."

Such audacious thoughts and hopes might haunt the spirit of the adept during the night following the mystic ceremony of resurrection. The following morning, in the avenues of the temple, beneath the blinding light, that night seemed to him no more than a dream . . . though how impossible to forget . . . that first voyage into the intangible and invisible! Once again he read the inscription on the statue of Isis: "My veil no mortal hand hath raised." All the same a corner of the veil was raised, but only to fall back again, and he woke up on the earth of tombs. Ah, how far he was from the goal he had dreamed of! For the voyage on the barque of millions of years is a long one! But at least he had caught a faint glimpse of his final destination. Even though his vision of the other world were only a dream, a childish outline of his imagination, still obscured by the mists of earth, could he doubt that other consciousness he had felt being born in him, that mysterious double, that celestial ego which had appeared to him in his astral beauty like a living form and spoken to him in his sleep? Was this a sister-soul, was it his genius, or only a reflection of his inmost spirit, a vision of his future being dimly foreshadowed? A wonder and a mystery! Surely it was a reality, and if that soul was only his own, it was the true one. What would he not do to recover it? Were he to live millions of years he would never forget that divine hour in which he had seen his other self, so pure and radiant.[54]

The initiation was at an end, and the adept consecrated as priest of Osiris. If he was an Egyptian, he remained attached to the temple; if a foreigner, he was permitted, from time to time, to return to his own country, therein to establish the worship of Isis or to accomplish a mission.

Before leaving, however, he swore a formidable oath that he would maintain absolute silence regarding the secrets of the temple. Never would he betray to a single person what he had seen or heard, never would he reveal the doctrine of Osiris except under the triple veil of the mythological symbols or of the mysteries. Were he to violate this oath, sudden death would come to him, sooner or later, however far away he might be. Silence, however, had become the buckler of his might.

On returning to the shores of Ionia, to the turbulent town in which he formerly lived, amidst that multitude of men, a prey to mad passions, who exist like fools in their ignorance of themselves, his thoughts often flew back to Egypt and the pyramids to the temple of Amon-Râ. Then the dream of the crypt came back to memory. And just as the lotus, in that distant land, spreads out its petals on the waves of the Nile, so this white vision floated above the slimy, turbulent stream of this life.

At chosen hours, he would hear its voice, and it was the voice of light. Arousing throughout his being the strains of an inner music, it said to him: "The soul is a veiled light. When neglected, it flickers and dies out, but when it is fed with the holy oil of love, it shines forth like an immortal lamp."

Footnotes

52. The Vision of Hermes is found at the beginning of the books of Hermes Trismegistus, under the name of Poimandres. The ancient Egyptian tradition has come down to us only in a slightly changed Alexandrian form. It has been attempted here to constitute this important fragment of Hermetic doctrine in the sense of the lofty initiation and esoteric synthesis it represents.

53 It is unnecessary to state that these gods bore other names in the Egyptian

tongue. The seven cosmogonic gods, however, correspond with one another in all mythologies, in meaning and attributes. They have their common root in the ancient esoteric tradition. As the western tradition has adopted the Latin names, we keep them for greater clearness.

54. In the Egyptian teachings, man was considered in this life to have consciousness only of the animal and the rational soul, called hati and bai. The higher part of his being, the spiritual soul and the divine being, cheybi and kou, exist in him as unconscious.

CHAPTER VIII

THE STORY OF THE BOOK OF THOTH

Now Ahura was the wife of Nefer-ka-ptah, and their child was Merab; this was the name by which he was registered by the scribes in the House of Life. And Nefer-ka-ptah, though he was the son of the King, cared for naught on earth but to read the ancient records, written on papyrus in the House of Life or engraved on stone in the temples; all day and every day he studied the writings of the ancestors.

One day he went into the temple to pray to the gods, but when he saw the inscriptions on the walls he began to read them; and he forgot to pray, he forgot the gods, he forgot the priests, he forgot all that was around him until he heard laughter behind him. He looked round and a priest stood there, and from him came the laughter.

"Why laughest thou at me?" said Nefer-ka-ptah.

"Because thou readest these worthless writings," answered the priest. "If thou wouldest read writings that are worth the reading I can tell thee where the Book of Thoth lies hidden."

Then Nefer-ka-ptah was eager in his questions, and the priest replied, "Thoth wrote the Book with his own hand, and in it is all the magic in the world. If thou readest the first page, thou wilt enchant the sky, the earth, the abyss, the mountains, and the sea; thou wilt understand the language of the birds of the air, and thou wilt know what the creeping things of earth are saying, and thou wilt see the fishes from the darkest depths of the sea. And if thou readest the other page, even though thou wert dead and in the world of ghosts, thou couldest come back to earth in the form thou once hadst. And besides this, thou wilt see the sun shining in the sky with the full moon and the stars, and thou wilt behold the great shapes of the gods."

Then said Nefer-ka-ptah, "By the life of Pharaoh, that Book shall be mine. Tell me whatsoever it is that thou desirest, and I will do it for thee."

"Provide for my funeral," said the priest. "See that I am buried as a rich man, with priests and mourning women, offerings, libations, and incense. Then shall my soul rest in peace in the fields of Aalu. One hundred pieces of silver must be spent upon my burying."

Then Nefer-ka-ptah sent a fleet messenger to fetch the money, and he paid one hundred pieces of silver into the priest's hands. When the priest had taken the silver, he said to Nefer-ka-ptah:

> *"The Book is at Koptos in the middle of the river.*
> *In the middle of the river is an iron box,*
> *In the iron box is a bronze box,*
> *In the bronze box is a keté-wood box,*

In the keté-wood box is an ivory-and-ebony box,
In the ivory-and-ebony box is a silver box,
In the silver box is a gold box,
And in the gold box is the Book of Thoth,

Round about the great iron box are snakes and scorpions and all manner of crawling things, and above all there is a snake which no man can kill. These are set to guard the Book of Thoth."

When the priest had finished speaking, Nefer-ka-ptah ran out of the temple, for his joy was so great that he knew not where he was. He ran quickly to Ahura to tell her about the Book and that he would go to Koptos and find it.

But Ahura was very sorrowful, and said, "Go not on this journey, for trouble and grief await thee in the southern land."

She laid her hand upon Nefer-ka-ptah as though she would hold him back from the sorrow that awaited him. But he would not be restrained, and broke away from her and went to the king his father.

He told the King all that he had learned, and said, "Give me the royal barge, O my father, that I may go to the southern land with my wife Ahura and my son Merab. For the Book of Thoth I must and will have."

So the King gave orders and the royal barge was prepared, and in it Nefer-ka-ptah, Ahura, and Merab sailed up the river to the southern land as far as Koptos. When they arrived at Koptos, the high priest and all the priests of Isis of Koptos came down to the river to welcome Nefer-ka-ptah, sacrificed an ox and a goose, and poured a libation of wine to Isis of Koptos and her son Harpocrates. After this, the priests of Isis and their wives made a great feast for four days in honor of Nefer-ka-ptah and Ahura.

On the morning of the fifth day, Nefer-ka-ptah called to him a priest of Isis, a great magician learned in all the mysteries of the gods. And together they made a little magic box, like the cabin of a boat, and they made men and a great store of tackle, and put the men and the tackle in the magic cabin. Then they uttered a spell over the cabin, and the men breathed and were alive, and began to use the tackle. And Nefer-ka-ptah sank the magic cabin in the river, saying "Workmen, workmen! Work for me!" And he filled the royal barge with sand and sailed away alone, while Ahura sat on the bank of the river at Koptos, and watched and waited, for she knew that sorrow must come of this journey to the southern land.

The magic men in the magic cabin toiled all night and all day for three nights and three days along the bottom of the river; and when they stopped the royal barge stopped also, and Nefer-ka-ptah knew that he had arrived where the Book lay hidden.

He took the sand out of the royal barge and threw it into the water, and it made a gap in the river, a gap of a schoenus long and a schoenus wide; in the middle of the gap lay the iron box, and beside the box was coiled the great snake that no man can kill, and all around the box on every side to the edge of the walls of water were snakes and scorpions and all manner of crawling things.

Then Nefer-ka-ptah stood up in the royal barge, and across the water he cried to the snakes and scorpions and crawling things; a loud and terrible cry, and the words were words of magic. As soon as his voice was still, the snakes and scorpions and crawling things were still also, for they were enchanted by means of the magical words of Nefer-ka-ptah, and they could not move. Nefer-ka-ptah brought the royal barge to the edge of the gap, and he walked through the snakes and scorpions and crawling things, and they looked at him, but could not move because of the spell that was on them.

And now Nefer-ka-ptah was face to face with the snake that no man could kill, and it reared itself up ready for battle. Nefer-ka-ptah rushed upon it and cut off its head, and at once the head and body came together, each to each, and the snake that no man could kill was alive again, and ready for the fray. Again Nefer-ka-ptah rushed upon it, and so hard did he strike that the head was flung far from the body, but at once the head and body came together again, each to each, and again the snake that no man could kill was alive and ready to fight. Then Nefer-ka-ptah saw that the snake was immortal and could not be slain but must be overcome by subtle means. Again he rushed upon it and cut it in two, and very quickly he put sand on each part, so that when the head and body came together there was sand between them and they could not join, and the snake that no man could kill lay helpless before him.

Then Nefer-ka-ptah went to the great box where it stood in the gap in the middle of the river, and the snakes and scorpions and crawling things watched, but they could not stop him.

> He opened the iron box and found a bronze box,
> He opened the bronze box and found a keté-wood box,
> He opened the keté-wood box and found an ivory-and-ebony box,
> He opened the ivory-and-ebony box and found a silver box,
> He opened the silver box and found a gold box,
> He opened the gold box and found the Book of Thoth.

He opened the Book and read a page, and at once he had enchanted the sky, the earth, the abyss, the mountains, and the sea, and he understood the language of birds, fish, and beasts. He read the second page and he saw the sun shining in the sky, with the full moon and the stars, and he saw the great shapes of the gods themselves; and so strong was the magic that the fishes came up from the darkest depths of the sea. So he knew that what the priest had told him was true.

Then he thought of Ahura waiting for him at Koptos, and he cast a magic spell upon the men that he had made, saying, "Workmen, workmen! Work for me! and take me back to the place from which I came." They toiled day and night till they came to Koptos, and there was Ahura sitting by the river, having eaten nothing and drunk nothing since Nefer-ka-ptah went away. For she sat waiting and watching for the sorrow that was to come upon them.

But when she saw Nefer-ka-ptah returning in the royal-barge, her heart was glad and she rejoiced exceedingly. Nefer-ka-ptah came to her and put the Book of Thoth into her hands and bade her read it. When she read the first page, she enchanted the sky, the earth, the abyss, the mountains, and the sea, and she understood the language of birds, fish, and beasts; and when she read the second page, she saw the sun shining in the sky, with the full moon and the stars, and she saw the great shapes of the gods themselves; and so strong was the magic that the fishes came up from the darkest depths of the sea.

Nefer-ka-ptah now called for a piece of new papyrus and for a cup of beer; and on the papyrus he wrote all the spells that were in the Book of Thoth. Then he took the cup of beer and washed the papyrus in the beer, so that all the ink was washed off and the papyrus became as though it had never been written on. And Nefer-ka-ptah drank the beer, and at once he knew all the spells that had been written on the papyrus, for this is the method of the great magicians. Then Nefer-ka-ptah and Ahura went to the temple of Isis and gave offerings to Isis and Harpocrates, and made a great feast, and the next day they went on board the royal barge and sailed joyfully away down the river towards the northern land.

But behold, Thoth had discovered the loss of his Book, and Thoth raged like a panther of the south, and he hastened before Ra and told him all, saving, "Nefer-ka-ptah has found my magic box and opened it, and has stolen my Book, even the Book of Thoth; he slew the guards that surrounded it, and the snake that no man can kill lay helpless before him. Avenge me, O Ra, upon Nefer-ka-ptah, son of the King of Egypt."

The majesty of Ra answered and said, "Take him and his wife and his child, and do with them as thou wilt." And now the sorrow for which Ahura watched and waited was about to come upon them, for Thoth took with him a power from Ra to give him his desire upon the stealer of his Book.

As the royal barge sailed smoothly down the river, the little boy Merab ran out from the shade of the awning and leaned over the side watching the water. And the power of Ra drew him, so that he fell into the river and was drowned. When he fell, all the sailors on the royal barge and all the people walking on the river-bank raised a great cry, but they could not save him. Nefer-ka-ptah came out of the cabin and read a magical spell over the water, and the body of Merab came to the surface and they brought it on board the royal barge. Then Nefer-ka-ptah read another spell, and so great was its power that the dead child spoke and told Nefer-ka-ptah all that had happened among the gods, that Thoth was seeking vengeance, and that Ra had granted him his desire upon the stealer of his Book.

Nefer-ka-ptah gave command, and the royal barge returned to Koptos, that Merab might be buried there with the honor due to the son of a prince. When the funeral ceremonies were over, the royal barge sailed down the river toward the northern land. A joyful journey was it no longer, for Merab was dead, and Ahura's heart was heavy on account of the sorrow that was still to come, for the vengeance of Thoth was not yet fulfilled.

They reached the place where Merab had fallen into the water, and Ahura came out from under the shade of the awning, and she leaned over the side of the barge, and the power of Ra drew her so that she fell into the river and was drowned. When she fell, all the sailors in the royal barge and all the people walking on the river-bank raised a great cry, but they could not save her. Nefer-ka-ptah came out of the cabin and read a magical spell over the water, and the body of Ahura came to the surface, and they brought it on board the royal barge. Then Nefer-ka-ptah read another spell and so great was its power that the dead woman spoke and told Nefer-ka-ptah all that had happened among the gods, that Thoth was still seeking vengeance, and that Ra had granted him his desire upon the stealer of his Book.

Nefer-ka-ptah gave command and the royal barge returned to Koptos, that Ahura might be buried there with the honor due to the daughter of a king. When the funeral ceremonies were over, the royal barge sailed down the river towards the northern land. A sorrowful journey was it now, for Ahura and Merab were dead, and the vengeance of Thoth was not yet fulfilled.

They reached the place where Ahura and Merab had fallen into the water, and Nefer-ka-ptah felt the power of Ra drawing him. Though he struggled against it he knew that it would conquer him. He took a piece of royal linen, fine and strong, and made it into a girdle, and with it he bound the Book of Thoth firmly to his breast, for he was resolved that Thoth should never have his Book again.

Then the power drew him yet more strongly, and he came from under the shade of the awning and threw himself into the river and was drowned. When he fell, all the sailors of the royal barge and all the people walking on the river-bank raised a great cry, but they could not save him. And when they looked for his body they could not find it. So the royal barge sailed down the river till they reached the northern land and came to Memphis, and the chiefs of the royal barge went to the king and told him all that had happened.

The king put on mourning raiment; he and his courtiers, the high priest and all the priests of Memphis, the king's army and the king's household, were clothed in mourning apparel, and they walked in procession to the haven of Memphis to the royal barge. When they came to the haven, they saw the body of Nefer-ka-ptah floating in the water beside the barge, close to the great steering-oars. And this marvel came to pass because of the magical powers of Nefer-ka-ptah; even in death he was a great magician by reason of the spells he had washed off the papyrus and drunk in the beer.

Then they drew him out of the water, and they saw the Book of Thoth bound to his breast with the girdle of royal linen. And the king gave command that they should bury Nefer-ka-ptah with the honor due to the son of a king, and that the Book of Thoth should be buried with him.

Thus was the vengeance of Thoth fulfilled, but the Book remained with Nefer-ka-ptah.

Parchment Books is committed to publishing high quality
Esoteric/Occult classic texts at a reasonable price.

With the premium on space in modern dwellings, we also strive - within the limits of good book design - to make our products as slender as possible, allowing more books to be fitted into a given bookshelf area.

Parchment Books is an imprint of Aziloth Books, which has established itself as a publisher boasting a diverse list of powerful, quality titles, including novels of flair and originality, and factual publications on controversial issues that have not found a home in the rather staid and politically-correct atmosphere of many publishing houses.

Titles Include:

The Interior Castle	St Teresa of Avila
The Everlasting Man	G K Chesterton
Heaven and Hell	Emanuel Swedenborg
The Signature of All Things	Jacob Boehme
Psychic Self-Defence	Dion Fortune
The Ancient Wisdom	Annie Besant
The Masters and the Path	C W Leadbeater
Man, His True Nature & Ministry	Louis-Claude de St.-Martin
Secret Doctrines of the Rosicrucians	Magus Incognito
Corpus Hermeticum	(trans. GRS Mead)
The Virgin of the World	Hermes Trismegistus
Raja Yoga	Yogi Ramacharaka
Theosophy	Rudolf Steiner
The Gospel of Thomas	Anonymous
Pistis Sophia	(trans. GRS Mead)
The Secret Destiny of America	Manly P Hall
Practical Mysticism	Evelyn Underhill
The Rosicrucian Mysteries	Max Heindel
The Conference of Birds	Farid ud-Din Attar
Meetings With Remarkable Men	G I Gurdjieff
War Is A Racket	Maj.-General Smedley D. Butler

Obtainable at all good online and local bookstores.
View Parchment Books' full list at: www.azilothbooks.com

We are a small, approachable company and would love to hear any of your comments and suggestions on our plans, products, or indeed on absolutely anything.   Aziloth is also interested in hearing from aspiring authors whom we might publish. We look forward to meeting you. Contact us at:

info@azilothbooks.com.

CATHEDRAL CLASSICS

Parchment Book's sister imprint, Cathedral Classics, hosts an array of classic literature, from ancient tomes to twentieth-century masterpieces, all of which deserve a place in your home. A small selection is detailed below:

Mary Shelley	*Frankenstein*
H G Wells	*The Time Machine; The Invisible Man*
Niccolo Machiavelli	*The Prince*
Omar Khayyam	*The Rubaiyat of Omar Khayyam*
Joseph Conrad	*Heart of Darkness; The Secret Agent*
Jane Austen	*Persuasion; Northanger Abbey*
Oscar Wilde	*The Picture of Dorian Gray*
Voltaire	*Candide*
Bulwer Lytton	*The Coming Race*
Arthur Conan Doyle	*The Adventures of Sherlock Holmes*
John Buchan	*The Thirty-Nine Steps*
Friedrich Nietzsche	*Beyond Good and Evil*
George Eliot	*Silas Marner*
Henry James	*Washington Square*
Stephen Crane	*The Red Badge of Courage*
Ralph Waldo Emmerson	*Self-Reliance, and Other Essays, (series 1&2)*
Sun Tzu	*The Art of War*
Charles Dickens	*A Christmas Carol*
Fyodor Dostoyevsky	*The Gambler; The Double*
Virginia Wolf	*To the Lighthouse; Mrs Dalloway.*
Johann W Goethe	*The Sorrows of Young Werther*
Walt Whitman	*Leaves of Grass - 1855 edition*
Confucius	*Analects*
Anonymous	*Beowulf*
Anne Bronte	*Agnes Grey*
More	*Utopia*
Farid ud-Din Attar	*The Conference of Birds*
Jack London	*Call of the Wild*
Edwin A. Abbott	*Flatland*

full list at: www.azilothbooks.com

Obtainable at all good online and local bookstores.

.

www.ingramcontent.com/pod-product-compliance
Lightning Source LLC
Chambersburg PA
CBHW051253170626
46809CB00004B/1624